Scrapbook Borders, Corners & Titles

Fresh techniques and innovative ideas for designer pages

M

MEMORY
MAKERS
BOOKS

Executive Editor Kerry Arquette Founder Michele Gerbrandt

Senior Editor MaryJo Regier

Art Director Andrea Zocchi

Designer Nick Nyffeler

Production Artist Dawn Knutson

Craft Director Pam Klassen

Idea Editor Janetta Wieneke

Photographer Ken Trujillo

Contributing Photographers Marc Creedon, Tara Cruz, Brenda Martinez

Contributing Writer Anne Wilbur

Editorial Support Associate Editor Shannon Hurd, Dena Twinem

Hand Model Ann Kitayama

Featured Artists See Artist Index on page 95

Memory Makers® Scrapbook Borders, Corners & Titles
Copyright © 2003 Memory Makers Books
All rights reserved.

Published by Memory Makers Books, an imprint of F+W Publications, Inc.
12365 Huron Street, Suite 500, Denver, CO 80234
Phone 1-800-254-9124
First edition. Manufactured in the United States of America

07 06 05 04   5 4 3

Library of Congress Cataloging-in-Publication Data

Scrapbook borders, corners & titles : fresh techniques and innovative ideas for designer pages.
    p. cm.
Includes bibliographical references.
ISBN 1-892127-13-X
    1. Photograph albums. 2. Photographs--Conservation and restoration. 3. Scrapbooks. I.
Title: Scrapbook borders, corners, and titles. II. Memory Makers Books.

TR465.S39 2003
745.593--dc21

                                                                              2002044449

Distributed to trade and art markets by
F+W Publications, Inc.
4700 East Galbraith Road, Cincinnati, OH 45236
Phone 1-800-289-0963

ISBN 1-892127-13-X

Memory Makers Books is the home of *Memory Makers*, the scrapbook magazine dedicated to educating and inspiring scrapbookers. To subscribe, or for more information, call 1-800-366-6465.
Visit us on the Internet at www.memorymakersmagazine.com

This book belongs to

We dedicate this book to all of our *Memory Makers* contributors whose fun and creative scrapbook page accents are the inspiration behind these pages.

Table of Contents

12 Winter

30 Spring

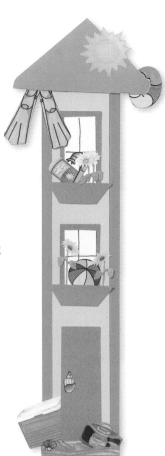

summertime is...

FAMILY

time

JULY 2002

Daniel, Anna, Michele, Ron, & Sasha

Introduction

Over the past decade I have seen my share of scrapbook pages, and generally they consist of three elements: a title, photos and journaling. Beyond these components are the embellishments that accessorize the page. Although it is true that over-accessorizing a page can take the focus away from the photos and journaling, when in balance embellishments can enhance the story behind the photos and allow for personal creativity.

In this book, we inspire scrapbookers with fresh and fun ensembles of page borders, corners and title designs for seasonal and holiday themes—including a peeking snowman, pierced egg die cuts, fiber-hung seed packets, and stamped and lacquered pumpkins, just to name a few.

Each and every scrapbook page featured also represents a different scrapbook technique, such as embossing with buttons or intaglio shrink art. Once you learn a technique, it can be applied to your own pages using relevant colors and themes to match your photos. Best of all, these custom-coordinated page accents will help you get more use out of your existing tools and supplies in ways that you may have never imagined.

This book also includes a basic list of tools and supplies, followed by helpful hints for working with color and adding texture and dimension. Each chapter represents a season and begins with an inspirational gallery of page ideas featured within the chapter. In addition, useful tips are sprinkled throughout and original patterns are provided.

All of these techniques are simple and easily mastered. So get out your scrapbook supplies and begin! Above all else, enjoy creating and personalizing your pages.

Michele

Michele Gerbrandt

Founding Editor

Memory Makers magazine

Basic tools & supplies

The following tools and supplies are used to create many of the scrapbook page projects featured in this book, although not every tool listed is used in every project. Before you begin any project, start with a clean work space that is covered with a self-healing cutting mat. Then assemble the following tools, depending on the project you've selected:

$\frac{1}{16}$", $\frac{1}{8}$" and $\frac{1}{4}$" round circle or hand punches

Beading needle

Black journaling pen

Bone folder

Button shank remover

Craft knife

Decorative scissors

Embossing heat gun

Embossing stylus

Eyelet setter and hammer

Metal straightedge ruler

Mouse pad or sheet of craft foam

Personal paper trimmer

Piercing awl or sewing needle

Round needle-nose pliers

Scissors

Small paintbrush

Small, stiff brush

Stabilo pencil

Tweezers

Adhesives

Your choice of adhesive is a personal preference, but the following wet and dry adhesives are used in this book—depending on the project featured—because each is best suited for different types of tasks. Photo-safe, acid-free adhesive products are recommended.

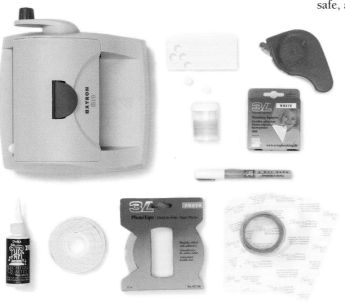

Adhesive application machine

Bottled glue

Double-sided foam tape

Double-sided photo tape

Double-sided sheet adhesive

Glue Dots®

Glue pen

Photo splits

Powder adhesive

Self-adhesive foam spacers

Tape roller

Other tools

The following tools are unique to a number of the projects in this book. If you don't have the specific tool we used, simply substitute your own tools as your page theme dictates.

Inkworkx® bulb sprayer

Lettering templates

Punches

QuicKutz™ letter press

Reproducible patterns (see pages 88-92)

Rubber stamps

Sizzix® die-cut machine

Paper

All projects featured use colored cardstock and/or patterned paper, as the foundation of the scrapbook page. When selecting paper colors, take the lead from your photos. Select 2-4 colors in the photos that best highlight the important aspects of the pictures, plus a neutral color—such as black, white or cream.

To help your photos "pop" off of the page, select lighter colored papers for photos with dark backgrounds and darker papers for photos with light backgrounds.

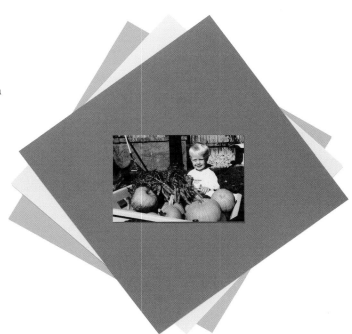

Colorants

Projects may also use one or more of the following colorants to add sizzle to the pages:

Black and colored pigment pens

Chalk

Clear and colored 3-D crystal lacquer

Clear embossing ink

Embossing pen

Embossing powders

Glitter

Glitter glue

Metal flake

Stamping inks

Watercolor paints

White opaque pen

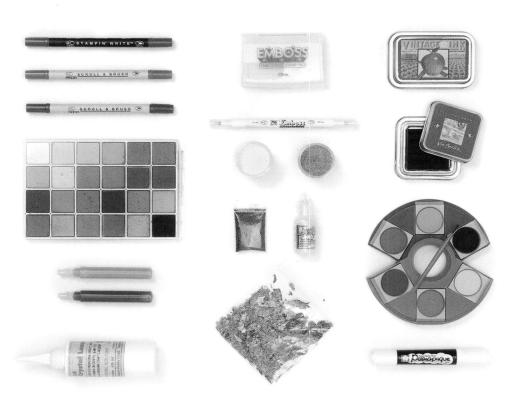

Other craft supplies

For texture and dimension, these craft supplies are used in one or more of the projects showcased:

Metallics

Eyelets

Fasteners

Wire

Wire mesh

Baubles

Flat and shank buttons

Seed and bugle beads

Sequins

Shaved ice®

Tiny glass marbles

Design additions

Die cuts

Paperclay®

Pre-made tags

Shimmer Sheetz®

Shrink plastic

Stickers

Organics

Pressed flowers

Tiny shells and starfish

Textiles

Embroidery floss

Fibers

Jute

Paper cord

Paper yarn

Raffia

String

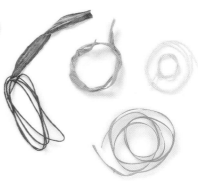

Winter

The warm memories, chilly fun and holiday happenings of wintertime are brimming with photo opportunities for scrapbookers! Make the perfect designer-look accents for those photos with:

• Progressive punch scenes • A window shaker box • Sticker reflections
• A peek-a-boo window • Embossed ornaments • Vellum stained glass
• Frosted letters • Threaded accents

These easy-to-learn techniques will give you plenty of ideas for year-round scrapbooking pleasure!

Progressive Punches
LAYER CHANGING SCENES

Joan Gosling, Keizer, Oregon

This technique, which resembles subsequent frames in a motion picture, can be used to represent a variety of activities such as building a snowman, constructing a home or planting a garden. Try other punched shapes or small die cuts to fit your page theme. Create the punched border and title as shown on the facing page. Mount border on left side of navy background. Fold photo corners from ¾ x 1½" navy strips. Slip corners onto photo and mount on a 6¼ x 4¼" evergreen mat. Mat again with white. Print and cut out caption. Double mat photo and caption together with navy and white paper. Add mini and small punched snowflakes embellished with glitter. Mount title centered above photo. Stamp letters for "fresh" on white paper and double mat.

MATERIALS

- Two sheets of navy solid-colored paper
- One sheet each of white and evergreen solid-colored paper
- Scraps of yellow and tan paper
- Super jumbo contemporary tree punch (Emagination Crafts)
- Mini snowflakes from snowflake corner rounder punch (Family Treasures)
- Tiny stars from bunting border, small circle and small snowflake punches (Marvy/Uchida)
- Lettering template (Provo Craft)
- Glitter glue (Ranger)
- Letter stamps (PSX Design)
- Navy stamping ink

1 Punch four evergreen and three white trees. Cut four 2¼ x 2½" navy rectangles. Freehand cut wavy strips of brown and white paper for the earth, snow and clouds.

2 Use scissors to trim off the bottoms of the white trees—about two thirds of the first tree, half of the second and a quarter of the third to represent the snowfall progression.

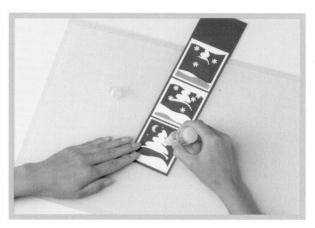

3 Layer trees with earth, snow and clouds on each navy rectangle. Punch yellow moons and stars and mini snowflakes. Mat each rectangle with white paper. Mount the rectangles in order on a 2¾" evergreen strip.

4 Use glitter glue to add sparkle to snow, stars and snowflakes.

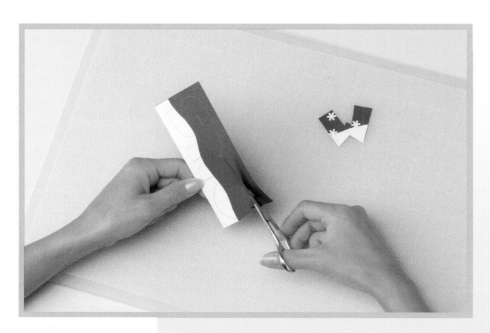

5 To create the title, mount a wavy white strip at the bottom of a navy strip. The widths of the strips depend upon the desired height of each letter. Use a lettering template to cut out each letter, positioning the snow at the bottom of each character. Accent with punched and trimmed mini snowflakes. Embellish with glitter. Mat each letter with evergreen and mount on a 7 x 2" strip of vellum.

Window Shaker Box

ENCASE GLITTERY SNOWFLAKES

Jodi Amidei, Lafayette, Colorado
Inspired by Teresa Magill

MATERIALS

- Window pattern on page 89
- One to two sheets each of cream and dusty blue solid-colored paper
- One sheet of patterned paper (MiniGraphics)
- Background stamp (Magenta)
- Black stamping ink
- Colored pens
- Glitter glue (Duncan Enterprises)
- Double-sided foam tape (3M)
- Scraps of vellum paper
- Mini snowflake punch (Family Treasures)
- Small plastic snowflakes (Jesse James Co.)
- Clear Mylar or poly page protector
- White paint
- Mini framed photos (Joshua's)
- Lettering template (EK Success)
- Colonial corner pocket punch (Marvy/Uchida)

Regardless of the subject, window shaker boxes add whimsy and fun to any scrapbook page. Any small objects can be used in a shaker box. Try seashells for a beach theme, tiny confetti notes for a music theme or mini punched leaves for autumn. To replicate this page, build the window shaker box following the steps on the facing page; mount at the top of solid-colored background paper along with mini framed photos. Use a similar technique to create the shaker box for the initial title letters. Cut remaining title letters using template. Print caption. Mount photos on cream rectangle. Create cream photo corners using corner pocket and mini star punches. Draw details around title shaker box, title letters, photo corners and caption with blue pen.

1 Cut a 4 x 12" cream strip. To create the village scene, stamp two images side by side. Embellish scene with colored pens and glitter glue for snow.

2 Cut a 4 x 12" patterned strip. Make two photocopies of the window pattern on page 89. Center the first pattern on the patterned strip and use it to cut out the windowpane openings. Use the second pattern to cut out the window frame from the same color as the background.

3 Trim strips of double-sided foam tape the same width as the window grids. Adhere strips to the back of the patterned window. Outline the outer edges of the entire strip as well as the window and panes.

4 Remove the tape backing and mount the patterned window on the stamped village scene. Fill each window pane with punched vellum snowflakes and small plastic snowflakes.

5 To mimic the window glass, trace the outside edge of the solid-colored window frame onto a rigid piece of Mylar or plastic page protector and cut out. Mount this piece beneath the window frame. Add "frost" by brushing white paint on the back of the plastic. Then mount the window frame over the patterned window to seal the shaker box.

Sticker Reflections
CREATE AN ILLUSION WITH MIRROR-IMAGE STICKERS

Megan Schoepf, Panama City, Florida
Photos Kelly Angard, Highlands Ranch, Colorado

MATERIALS

- One sheet each of dark green, purple and lavender solid-colored paper
- One sheet of light blue solid-colored ribbed paper
- One sheet each of white and blue vellum paper (Karen Foster)
- Penguin and Winterscape stickers (Mrs. Grossman's)
- Glitter (Magic Scraps)
- Alphabet stickers (C-Thru Ruler)
- Black pen

You can use this technique with any sticker images that are mirror images along any line, whether vertical, horizontal or even diagonal. First create the penguin border as shown on the facing page. Use the same technique to create the title and an additional penguin accent. Mat border with purple paper and mount on left side of dark green background. Crop photos and mat with light blue ribbed paper. For corner accents, cut lavender triangles and embellish with glitter. Write caption on lavender rectangle.

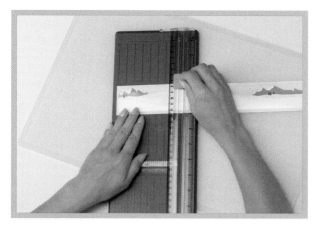

1 Cut a 3½ x 11½" rectangle of blue ribbed paper. Trim two 3½" sections of the Winterscape border sticker for the upper and lower parts of the border. Freehand cut additional vellum strips.

2 Cut a 3½" strip of blue vellum to overlay the border background; attach at lower edge using a snowy section of border sticker. Mount a white vellum strip over this sticker section. Pull back the vellum overlay and adhere mirror-image penguin stickers to the border background.

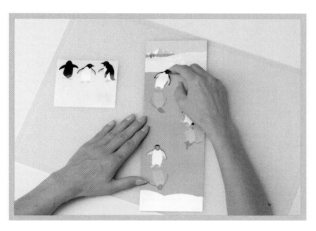

3 Attach the top of vellum overlay to the background using a mountain section of border sticker layered with a white vellum strip. Adhere matching penguin stickers on the vellum overlay to create the illusion of a reflection.

4 Use glue and glitter to accent snowbank and lake edges.

VARIATION

For a terrific take on a familiar fairy tale, assemble a princely reflection for a plain 'ol frog die cut (Ellison) using a Paperkins paper doll kit (EK Success) layered beneath blue vellum paper.

Megan Schoepf, Panama City, Florida

Peek-a-Boo Window
PEER THROUGH FROSTED PANES

There are no buddies like SNOW buddies

Deana, Sarah, Amanda, and Griffin
These four kids have been friends since 1984.
They have celebrated birthdays, build snowmen,
shot fireworks, and attended school together.

Linda Cummings, Murfreesboro, Tennessee

You can illustrate any season or activity using this window technique. Simply fill the window with the appropriate scene—a bunny for Easter, fireworks for the Fourth of July, a jack-o-lantern or ghost for Halloween or lighted trees for the holidays. For this wintry scene, first assemble the window as shown on the facing page. Mat photo with brown paper; cut triangles for corner accents and embellish with punched snowflakes. Print and mat caption and title, leaving extra space beneath the first title phrase. Use lettering template to cut larger title letters from patterned paper. For the letter mats, cut another set of brown letters. Layer letters slightly askew and mount with self-adhesive foam spacers.

MATERIALS

- Snowman, window and curtain patterns on page 89
- Scraps of white and orange solid-colored paper
- One sheet each of cream, brown and red solid-colored paper
- One sheet each of pine tree and brown check patterned paper (Frances Meyer, Rocky Mountain Scrapbook Co.)
- One sheet of patterned vellum paper (EK Success)
- Colored chalk
- White opaque, brown and black pens
- Large snowflake and small spiral punches (All Night Media, Family Treasures)
- Lettering template (C-Thru Ruler)
- Curlz MT computer font (fonts.com)
- Self-adhesive foam spacers

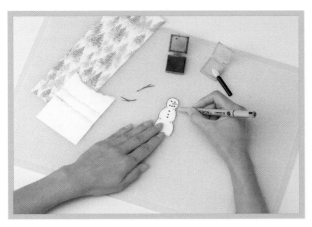

1 Use the pattern on page 89 to cut snowman shape. Draw details with black pen and shade with colored chalk. Cut brown twigs for arms and orange carrot for nose.

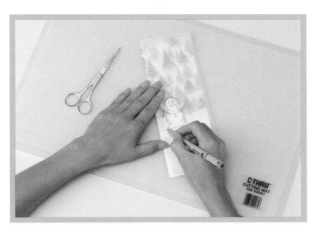

2 Cut a 3 x 9" rectangle of pine tree paper. Cut a matching rectangle of patterned vellum paper for the overlay. Lay the snowman in the desired position beneath the patterned vellum and on top of the pine tree background. Trace an oval around the snowman's face and part of his body. Cut out the oval opening.

3 Mount a scrap of plastic page protector or transparency film beneath the oval opening. Use an opaque white pen to add frost details to the back of the vellum overlay. Draw swishes and dots to simulate a frosted window. Mount vellum overlay over snowman on top of background.

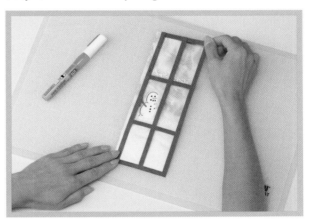

4 Cut ¼" brown strips for the window frame. Draw details with brown and black pens. Use the pattern to layer strips for the window frame.

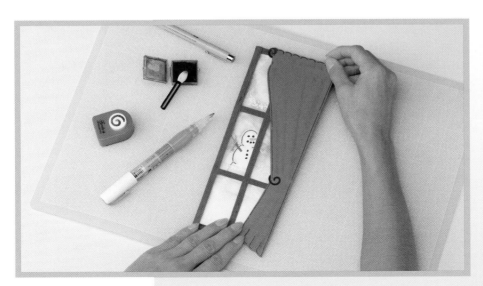

5 Use the pattern to cut the red curtain. Draw details with black pen and shade with chalk. Punch small black spirals for curtain rod and tie-back hardware.

Embossed Ornaments

IMPRESS RAISED IMAGES IN MYLAR SHEETS

how the boys **trim** *the* **tree**

Colt (14) reluctantly builds the tree.

Hunter (1½) test drives empty box.

Colt pulls stray needles from feet.

Jake (8½) and Dylan (12) decorate it!

MaryJo Regier, Littleton, Colorado

Take the garland idea to new "lengths" with different beads, buttons, bows and other embellishments. If you poke a hole in it, you can string it on a garland. Simply use different-themed shank buttons to fit your page theme. To create the embossed ornament garlands, follow the steps on the facing page. Position garlands on the left edge and lower right corner of trimmed plaid paper; tape ends on the backside. Double-mat plaid paper with white and evergreen. Crop and mat photos. Print and adhere captions. Print title, leaving space for large letters. Trim title to a ½" strip and mat with evergreen. Use templates to cut letters and numbers from Shimmer Sheetz; mat with evergreen; mount with self-adhesive foam spacers.

1 Use an embossing heat gun to heat Shimmer Sheetz. Move the heat gun in a circular motion for 10 to 15 seconds to evenly heat the material, which will become soft and pliable.

2 Lay the warmed Shimmer Sheetz on a mouse pad or three sheets of craft foam. Firmly push the patterned side of a Christmas button into the Shimmer Sheetz to emboss the button's design. Remove the button and allow the Shimmer Sheetz to cool.

3 Repeat Steps 1 and 2 until all desired images are embossed. Use small, sharp scissors to trim around the edges of each embossed ornament.

4 Use beading thread and a beading needle to string garlands of embossed ornaments and bugle beads.

MATERIALS

- One sheet plaid patterned paper (Hot Off The Press)
- Two sheets green solid-colored paper
- One sheet white solid-colored paper
- One sheet each of red and white iris Shimmer Sheetz (Sulyn Industries)
- Embossing heat gun
- Mouse pad or 3 sheets craft foam
- Christmas buttons (Blumenthal Lansing)
- Red and green bugle beads (Westrim)
- Beading thread and needle
- Lettering template (C-Thru Ruler)
- Self-adhesive foam spacers

Vellum Stained Glass

PIECE A LUMINOUS DESIGN

Jenna Beegle, Woodstock, Georgia

MATERIALS

- Pattern on page 88
- One sheet each of white and black solid-colored paper
- Scraps or small sheets of red, light green, dark green and yellow vellum paper
- Glue pen (Zig Two-Way from EK Success)
- Pebbles in My Pocket lettering template (EK Success)
- Black pen

Using a simple geometric design to create a border saves time without losing impact. Check your local library for thousands of different stained-glass patterns. To re-create this stained-glass border, follow the steps on the facing page. Mount border at bottom of white background. (If you choose a dark background, back the border with white paper.) Use the same technique to create stained-glass corner accents for caption and stained-glass letters for title. Double-mat photo with two shades of vellum paper. Pencil lines for caption and write with pencil; trace with thin black pen.

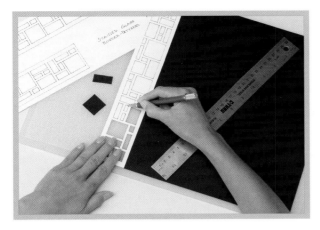

1 Make two photocopies of stained-glass window pattern. Place the first pattern over black paper on a cutting mat. Hold the pattern in place or secure it with removable tape. Cut out the window frame using a craft knife and a metal-edge ruler as needed.

2 Lay the second pattern beneath a piece of colored vellum paper. Trace the window panes you wish to fill with that color, making each pane slightly larger than the frame opening. Repeat for each color vellum. You can also use craft punches to punch rectangles and squares.

3 Use a glue pen to adhere each vellum pane to the back of the window frame.

VARIATION

A silver window frame and soft pastel vellum papers bring an entirely different feeling to the same window pattern. Change the lettering style simply by using a different lettering template (ScrapPagerz).

Jenna Beegle, Woodstock, Georgia

Frosted Letters
DECORATE SATISFYING SWEETS

Betsy Bell Sammarco, New Canaan, Connecticut

This title idea is perfect for those with an incurable sweet tooth. You'll have no trouble thinking up ways to embellish dozens of cookie letters for any holiday baking—including Valentine's Day, Easter and Halloween! For this Christmas title, cut and double mat a 2" strip of silver metallic paper; mount at top of red flecked background. Create cookie letters following the steps on the facing page. Snip the lower right corner of the letter S using Ripple scissors. Mount letters on title strip. For the large cookies, punch large hearts, stars and trees from brown and white Diamond Dust paper; trim white pieces and layer over brown. For the border design, cut six 1" silver squares and mount on left edge of page. Punch small stars, snowflakes, hearts and gingerbread men from brown paper; "frost" punched shapes by coloring with white opaque pen, leaving a brown border. Write caption on brown rectangle; shade with brown chalk. Crop and mat photos and caption. Accent photo corners with triangles and mini cookies. Embellish with additional seed beads.

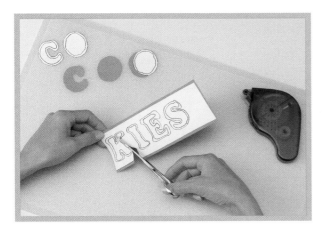

1 Make two photocopies of the lettering pattern. Lay the first pattern over a 2" brown strip. Hold pattern in place with removable tape. Cut out letters following the outer lines on the pattern.

2 Use brown chalk to shade the letter edges to resemble baked gingerbread cookies.

3 Place the second pattern over a 2" strip of white Diamond Dust paper. Hold pattern in place with removable tape. Cut out letters, this time following the inner lines of the pattern to form the frosting layer.

4 Mount white letters over brown letters. Use tweezers and a fine-tipped glue pen or bottle to adhere green and red seed beads to each letter.

MATERIALS

- Lettering pattern on page 89
- One sheet red flecked patterned paper (Keeping Memories Alive)
- One sheet gingerbread men patterned paper (The Paper Patch)
- One sheet silver metallic paper (Daler-Rowney Canford Paper)
- One sheet each of brown and red solid-colored paper
- One sheet white Diamond Dust paper (Paper Adventures)
- Red and green seed beads
- Small gingerbread man punch (EK Success)
- Small snowflake, star and heart, and large star, heart and fir tree punches (Marvy/Uchida)
- Ripple scissors (Fiskars)
- Colored chalk
- White opaque and black pens

Threaded Accents
STITCH AND WRAP PAGE EMBELLISHMENTS

Anissa Stringer, Phoenix, Arizona

This border and title idea takes little time but makes a big design impact. Best of all, it's easy to adapt to any theme. For the background, crumple a sheet of gold mulberry or handmade paper and flatten several times to achieve the desired texture. Create the wrapped tree, corner accents and title following the steps on the facing page. Write caption with gold pen on evergreen rectangle; wrap in the same manner as the tree. Crop photos. Mat all elements with dark red mulberry and arrange on gold background.

MATERIALS

- Tree pattern on page 89
- One sheet gold mulberry paper (source unknown)
- One sheet evergreen solid-colored paper
- One sheet dark red mulberry paper (PrintWorks)
- Scrap of brown paper
- ¾" square punch
- Star-shaped brad fasteners (HyGlo/AmericanPin)
- Gold metallic thread
- Sewing needle
- Gold metallic pen

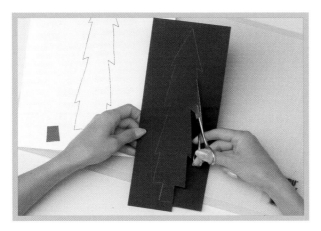

1 Photocopy tree pattern. Cut tree from evergreen paper and trunk section from brown paper. Punch evergreen squares for corner accents. Adhere star brad fasteners to tree and squares.

2 Wrap tree and evergreen squares with gold metallic thread. Secure ends on the backside with tape.

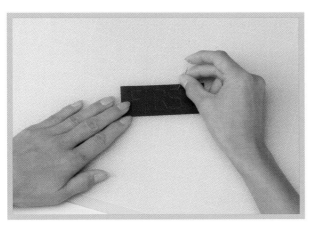

3 Freehand draw letters for title on 1¼" evergreen strips. Following the lines, use a sewing needle to pierce holes for stitching.

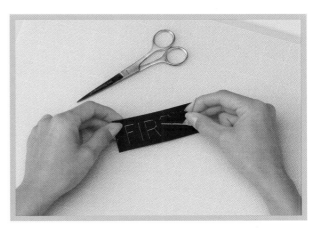

4 Thread sewing needle with gold metallic thread and stitch gold letters. Secure ends with tape on the back of the title strips.

VARIATION

Adapt the wrapped and sewn concept to a spring theme with a freehand-cut floral topiary and a "bunny pink" title stitched with embroidery floss. For fall, try leaves wrapped in bronze thread and orange stitched letters.

Anissa Stringer, Phoenix, Arizona

Spring

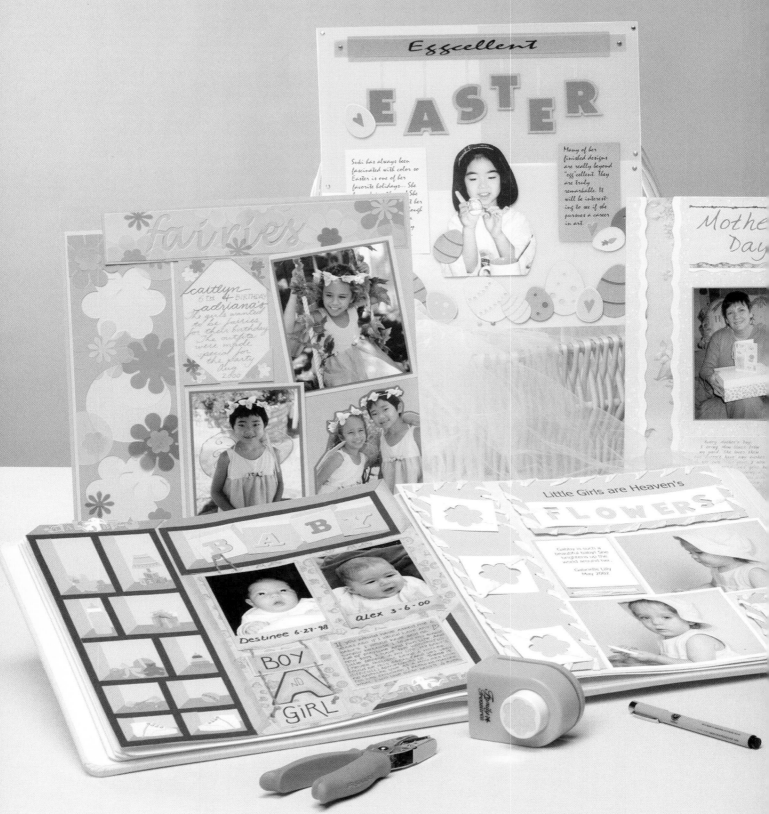

Memorable events fill our spring days—from the budding of green leaves that are brighter than any other time of the year and egg-painting to honoring Mother and dressing little girls in delicate dresses. Create the perfect page accents for your springtime photos with:

- Raffia lacing   • Folk hearts   • Layered shapes   • Stamped paper clay
- Cracked glass   • Pierced die cuts   • A shadow box   • Decorative edges

Once you've tried these simple scrapbook projects, you'll be racing to apply the ideas to your winter, summer and fall pages as well!

Raffia Lacing
WHIP STITCH TEXTURED EDGES

Terri Davenport, Toledo, Ohio

These laced borders, titles and corner accents are reminiscent of old-fashioned lacing cards, and they couldn't be easier to create. Just punch holes and stitch with paper raffia. Change the punched shape and the raffia color to fit your page theme. Refer to the instructions on the facing page to create the title, border and corner accent. Computer print the caption on white paper; trim and mat with pink. Punch two holes at the bottom of the caption and lace with white raffia. Mat photos with white paper. Arrange elements on a light pink background.

MATERIALS

- One sheet each of white, pink and light pink solid-colored paper
- Large flower punch (Family Treasures)
- Letter punches (EK Success)
- ⅛" hole punch
- White Twistel paper raffia (Making Memories)

1 Cut four 2" white squares. Punch centers with large flower punch. Cut a 1½ x 7" white strip for the title; punch letters, saving the centers of the O and R.

2 Print black title words on pink paper; trim to 3½ x 8". Cut two additional pink rectangles in these sizes: 3 x 11½" for the border and 2¾ x 3¼" for the corner piece. Use a pencil and a graphing ruler to mark dots along the edges of each rectangle. They should be about ¼" in from the edges and spaced about ¾" to 1" apart. Punch holes with ⅛" hole punch.

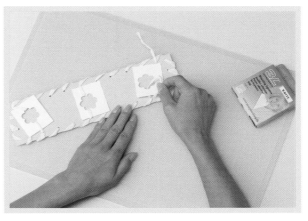

3 Lace the edges of each rectangle using a whip stitch. Simply pull the raffia up through one hole, wrap it around the edge of the rectangle and pull it up through the next hole. Be sure to lace through each hole in the same direction.

4 Use additional raffia to secure the title and white punched flowers to the pink rectangles. Use tape to secure all loose ends to the back of each rectangle. Mount the centers of the O and R on the title.

VARIATION

Lace up a little boy page by combining bright blue and pale sage paper with punched dragonflies (McGill). Use a lettering template (EK Success) to create the whimsical letters.

Terri Davenport, Toledo, Ohio

Folk Hearts

CONTRAST TEXTURED RAFFIA WITH SIMPLE GRAPHIC ELEMENTS

Nicole Hinrichs Ramsaroop, Horst, The Netherlands

Accented "banners" make for quick and easy page embellishments. To change the theme from "love", simply change the hearts to a different shape such as Easter eggs, flowers, leaves or Christmas trees and apply them to the banners. Start with a cream scrapbook page or a solid-colored background. For the background, mount a 10 x 12" sheet of plum paper next to a 2" strip of tan raffia. (Dampen the raffia to make it easier to untwist.) For the border background, mount a 1½" strip of untwisted tan raffia in the center of a 4 x 11½" red strip. Follow the steps on the facing page to create the hearts and banners. Mount banners on the border as shown. Cut a 4" red square in half to create the lower right triangle. Mount large heart over triangle. Use the computer font as a template for the large title letters; cut out and mat with plum mulberry. Write remaining title words with thick black pen on dark red strips; mat with tan paper. Crop and mat photos and printed caption. Draw details with black pen.

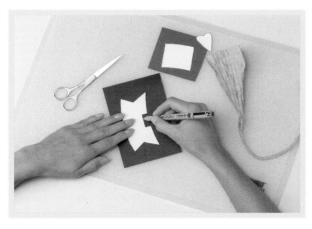

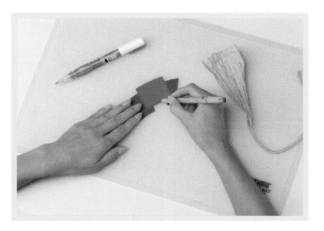

1 Photocopy and cut out heart and banner patterns (enlarge or reduce heart as needed; banner pattern has two pieces). Trace around each pattern piece onto the appropriate colors of paper and raffia. Cut one large heart, three small hearts and three of each banner piece.

2 Mount each rectangular piece onto each banner. Draw banner details with black pen.

3 Use a small paintbrush and water to lightly dampen mulberry paper. Place a raffia heart over the dampened mulberry and hold in place. Following the edges of the raffia heart, tear mulberry paper into a slightly larger heart shape. Repeat for each heart. Mount hearts onto mulberry mats.

4 Adhere hearts to banners. Punch a hole in the center of one small heart, punching through all layers. Punch a hole in the center of the large heart. Insert brad fasteners through holes and flatten ends on the backside.

MATERIALS

- Heart and banner patterns on page 91
- Cream scrapbook page or background paper
- One sheet each of red, dark red, plum and tan solid-colored paper
- Tan Twistel paper raffia (Making Memories)
- Plum mulberry paper (Bazzill)
- Gold-colored brad fasteners
- ⅛" hole punch
- Sk8 or Dye computer font (PizzaDude.dk)
- Black pens

Layered Shapes
COMBINE PUNCHED SHAPES AND OPENINGS

Pam Klassen, Westminster, Colorado
Photos Patricia Hymovitz, Torrance, California; Michele Rank,
Cerritos, California; JoDee Yamasaki, Torrance, California

All you need are a few geometric or organic-shaped punches to create striking page elements with depth and dimension. Here's your chance to experiment with different patterns, textures and color combinations for a truly one-of-a-kind look. Create the title and border following the steps on the facing page; mount on a bright pink background. Crop photos and mat using lime vellum and light pink paper. Write caption on light pink vellum rectangle; mount over white rectangle. Create corner accents using the same punching and layering technique as the border.

MATERIALS

- One sheet each of light green, lime green, bright pink and light pink solid-colored paper
- One sheet each of bright yellow, pink, dark pink and lime green vellum paper
- Medium flower and gigantic flower, groovy flower and 2¾" circle punches (Family Treasures)
- Medium daisy punch (Carl)
- Small flower and 2" circle punches (Emagination Crafts)
- Small flower punch (EK Success)
- Personal die-cutting system and letter dies (QuicKutz) or lettering template or letter punches
- Colored pens

1 Cut a 3⅝ x 11" light green strip. Punch gigantic groovy flower and 2" circle openings toward the right side.

2 Cut a 3⅜ x 10¾" bright pink strip. Punch gigantic flower and 2¾" circle openings so that they partially overlap the openings in the light green strip.

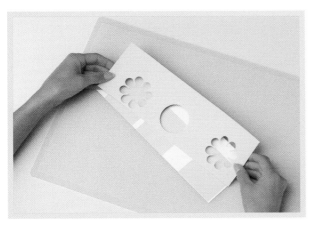

3 For the border backing, cut a white strip the same size as the light green strip. Mount squares of bright yellow vellum and pink paper beneath the openings in the light green strip. Mount the light green strip on the white backing.

4 Punch additional flowers from colored vellum and layer on the bright pink strip, trimming as necessary. To complete the border, mount the bright pink strip over the light green strip.

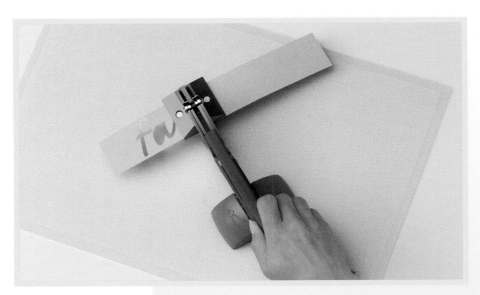

5 Follow the manufacturer instructions to die-cut the title letters in a 10¼ x 1¾" bright pink strip; mat with lime green; embellish with punched and trimmed vellum flowers and circles.

Stamped Paper Clay
REVERSE-EMBOSS WHIMSICAL IMAGES

Erikia Ghumm, Brighton, Colorado
Photos Catherine Medlin, Brighton, Colorado

MATERIALS

- One sheet of speckled green patterned paper (Provo Craft)
- One sheet of cream solid-colored paper
- Paper clay (Creative Paperclay Co.)
- Easter stamps (PSX Design)
- Watercolor paints
- Embroidery floss
- Purple pen

These paper tiles are created with Paperclay, an acid-free product that air dries in about a day. It is light-weight and can be rolled thin and embedded with beads or other embellishments. The product comes in a natural white color but can be painted when dry. Besides stamping, you can also use push molds, cookie cutters or form objects freehand. To create the reverse-embossed images, follow the steps on the facing page. To create the corner accents, simply roll out Paperclay to ⅛" thickness, cut into triangles, allow to dry, and paint with watercolors. Mount the paper-clay elements on a patterned background. Crop and mat photos. Write captions and draw details with purple pen.

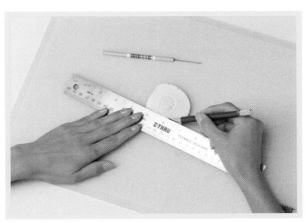

1 Use a small rolling pin or dowel to roll out paper clay to ⅛" thickness. Firmly press stamp into clay without rocking. Lift stamp straight up from clay. Repeat for each design. The clay now has reverse-embossed images.

2 Use a craft knife and metal ruler to cut the images into tile shapes. Use an awl to pierce a hole at the top and bottom of each title. Pierce a single hole in the *Happy Easter* tile.

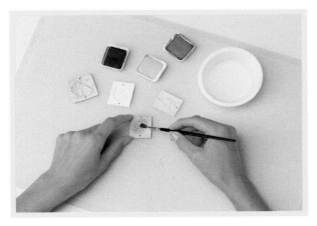

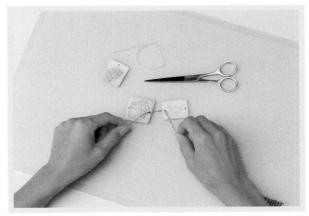

3 Let the paper clay dry overnight. Paint with a light coating of watercolor paint and allow to air dry.

4 Create a garland by tying the tiles together with colored strands of embroidery floss. String floss through the Happy Easter tile and tie a bow.

VARIATION

Change the look of this technique by inking the stamps before pressing them into the paper clay. Then tear the edges of each image. (School stamps by PSX Design, Stampcraft by Plaid Enterprises and Stampin' Up; papers by Scrapbook Wizard)

Erikia Ghumm, Brighton, Colorado
Photos Lora Mason, Orlando, Florida

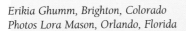

Cracked Glass
HEAT AND BEND ULTRA THICK EMBOSSING ENAMEL

Erikia Ghumm, Brighton, Colorado
Photos Sally Scamfer, Bellvue, Nebraska

MATERIALS

- Heart pattern on page 90
- One sheet of patterned paper (Anna Griffin)
- One sheet each of cream and tan solid-colored paper
- Journaling block (Anna Griffin)
- Purple pen
- Suze Weinberg's Clear Ultra Thick Embossing Enamel (Ranger)
- Clear embossing ink pad
- Embossing heat gun
- Pressed flowers (Nature's Pressed)
- Tweezers

Ultra thick embossing enamel is similar to regular embossing powder except that the grains are larger, which results in a thicker coating. This embossing technique can be used with any flat object such as stickers, duplicate photos, die cuts, punched shapes, stamped images and printed designs that coordinate with your page theme. Follow the steps on the facing page to create the cracked hearts. Use the same technique to create the photo corner accents and the title strip, which incorporates both pressed flowers and a handwritten label sticker. Double mat photo and center on patterned background. Adhere cracked glass accents with a strong adhesive.

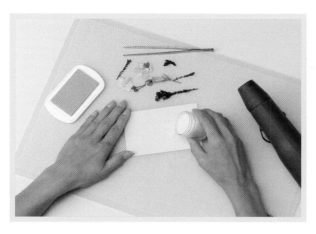

1 Stamp cream paper with clear embossing ink pad. Apply a layer of ultra thick embossing enamel (UTEE). Tap off excess. Heat with embossing gun about 2" from the surface until it melts.

2 Gently press a dried flower into the melted UTEE using tweezers. Allow to cool several minutes.

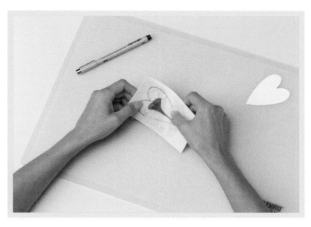

3 Stamp surface with clear embossing ink, apply another layer of UTEE, and heat surface again. Apply additional layers of UTEE while the previous layer is still hot until the image is the desired thickness.

4 Place heart pattern over the flower image and trace. Carefully holding the flower image in both hands, gently bend the paper to create the cracked-glass effect.

5 Cut out heart shape, cutting just inside the traced heart outline.

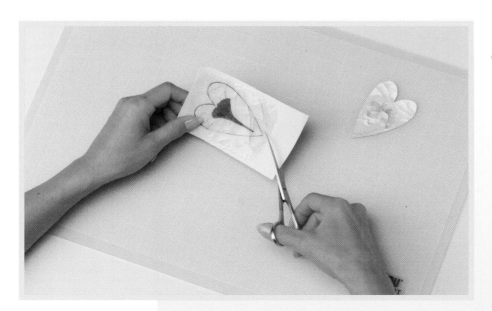

Pierced Die Cuts
OUTLINE SIMPLE SHAPES WITH TINY PINPRICKS

Sandi Genovese for Ellison Craft & Design
Photos Vicki Krum, Redmond, Washington

Paper piercing is an easy technique that adds texture and pattern to basic shapes and solid colors. First cut and piece vellum rectangles to fit on a white background. Adhere vellum corners at page center. Attach remaining vellum corners by punching holes and inserting mini brad fasteners. Print title on pink vellum; trim and mount over solid blue strip using mini brad fasteners. Silhouette-cut photo and mount with self-adhesive foam spacers. Print captions; accent with punched hearts and carrots. Follow the steps on the facing page to create the pierced title letters and eggs. Use self-adhesive foam spacers to mount letter die cuts; adhere vellum line stickers. Arrange eggs using self-adhesive foam spacers as desired.

1 Follow the manufacturer instructions to die cut letters and eggs from various shades of solid-colored papers. Select two shades of the same color for each egg.

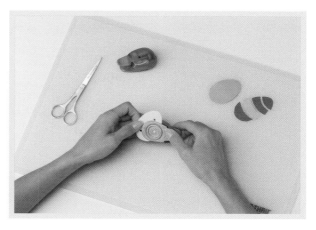

2 Choose one color for the top layer of each egg; punch various sizes of holes or cut apart into strips.

3 Use a sewing needle or straight pin to pierce designs around each punched hole. For the striped eggs, pierce holes along the edges of each stripe or in the lower layer between stripes. For the letter die cuts, pierce holes in the larger letter mats around the smaller letters.

4 Assemble egg layers and accent with punched carrots and hearts. Pierce additional holes as desired.

MATERIALS

- One sheet white paper for background
- One sheet each of yellow, green, blue and pink colored vellum (Hot Off The Press)
- Shades of yellow, green, blue, pink and orange solid-colored paper
- Mini brad fasteners (Making Memories)
- Sizzix personal die-cutting system, alphabet and eggs dies (Ellison/Provo Craft), or letter and egg templates
- Large egg die cuts (Ellison)
- $7/16$" and $3/16$" hole punches
- Heart and carrot punches (EK Success)
- Needle or straight pin
- Vellum line stickers (Mrs. Grossman's)
- Self-adhesive foam spacers

Shadow Box
CONNECT SOLID STRIPS FOR A DIMENSIONAL EFFECT

Nicole Hinrichs Ramsaroop
Horst, The Netherlands

It's not difficult to imagine all sorts of treasures to place in these shadow box designs. How about seashells, potted plants, Christmas ornaments, paper dolls or actual dollhouse miniatures? For this baby theme, first layer patterned paper on a cream background. Follow the steps on the facing page to create the shadow box for the border. Use the same technique to create the title shadow box, blocks for sticker letters and a corner embellishment. Crop and mat photos, tearing lower mat edges and shading with colored chalk. Write titles and caption; shade with chalk; cut out and mat. Punch holes in titles and connect with blue twine. Attach solid blue eyelet at top loop of twine.

1 Transfer shadow box patterns to gray paper, or trace patterns onto gray paper using a light box. Cut ½" dark blue strips for the face, ½" light blue strips for the sides and ½" medium blue strips for the shelves.

2 Using the pattern lines as a guide, trim and mount strips to create the shadow box. Miter the corners as shown to give the illusion of depth.

3 Trim additional ½" strips for the top and right sides. Arrange these pieces with the shadow box on the page background. Shade the right side with blue chalk.

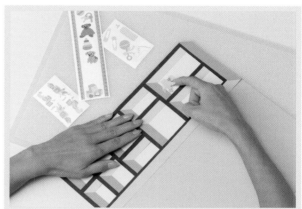

4 Decorate the shadow box with stickers.

MATERIALS

- Shadow box patterns on page 90
- Cream scrapbook page or background paper
- One sheet of blue patterned paper (Current)
- One sheet each of gray, dark blue, medium blue, light blue, pink, lavender and mint green solid-colored paper
- Colored chalk
- Various stickers related to page theme (Mrs. Grossman's)
- Black pens
- ⅟₁₆" hole punch
- Blue twine
- Solid blue eyelet

Decorative Edges
LAYER PERFECTLY MATCHED STRIPS

Pamela Frye, Denver, Colorado

This technique is so versatile that it's difficult to think of a theme with which it won't work. Vary the look by changing the style of decorative scissors and patterned papers. For this spring page, follow the steps on the facing page to create the border. Crop and mat photos. Cut triangles for corner accents; trim with decorative scissors and layer as shown. Print title, year and caption. Trim lower edges of title and year with decorative scissors. Double mat title with printed vellum and white paper. Embellish caption and title with purple fiber.

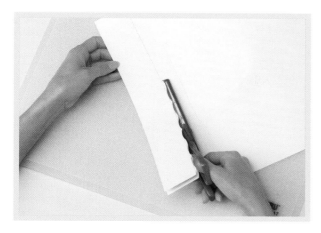

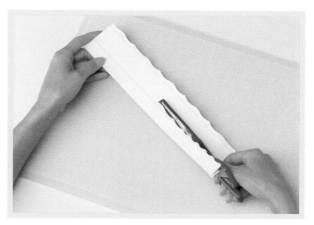

1 The key to lining up decorative edges is to cut the paper layers together. To do so, use removable tape to adhere a 6" strip of white paper to the back of a sheet of patterned paper. Use a pencil and ruler to draw a cutting guideline about 2" from one edge. Cut along the guideline with decorative scissors. Lay aside the larger piece and use the remaining border strip for Step 2.

2 Draw a second cutting guideline on the border strip parallel to the first cut line and about ½" from the straight edge. Cut along this second guideline with decorative scissors. Save the strips with two decorative edges for the corner and title accents.

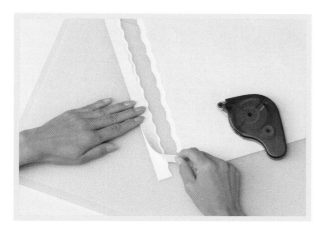

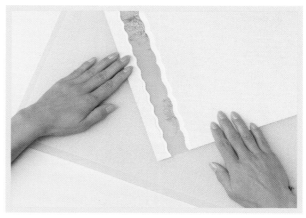

3 Remove tape and separate layers of white and patterned paper. Mat cut edge of narrow patterned strip with matching white strip. Mat cut edge of patterned page with matching white strip.

4 Cut a 2" strip of printed embossed vellum. Using a full sheet of white paper as a base, layer this strip between the decorative edges to complete the border design.

MATERIALS

- One sheet white paper for the background
- One sheet yellow patterned paper
  (Scrapbook Wizard)
- One sheet each of white, lavender and
  purple solid-colored paper
- One sheet of Juliana Lilacs printed embossed vellum
  (K & Company)
- Decorative scissors
- Purple fiber (On the Surface)

Summer

The sun is out, the breeze is warm, and there's tons to do outdoors! Family vacations, tending the garden, water play, and trips to the zoo are the joys of summer. Capture the frolicking activities on film and preserve them on pages that include:

- Marbled designs • Fancy vegetables • Tied tags • Intaglio shrink art
- Knotted twine • Twisted wire • String-tie and brad fasteners • Layered scenes
- Embellished edges

These clever and oh-so-cute concepts will provide you with hours of seasonal scrapbook fun. The hard part will be determining to which season you want to apply the concepts next!

Marbled Designs

GLUE TINY GLASS MARBLES FOR A BUMPY EFFECT

Suzee Gallagher, Villa Park, California

The texture of these marbled embellishments is so appealing that you just have to rub your fingers over the smooth yet bumpy surface. This is a great technique for bringing dimension to pre-printed punch outs and die cuts, stickers and clip art. For the background of this summer theme, mat a trimmed sheet of green paper with yellow. Print caption. Triple mat photo. Create the title and border as shown on the facing page. Apply letters, bugs and other designs to title, border, caption and photo corners using self-adhesive foam spacers as desired.

1 Punch out the desired printed designs. Select the areas that you wish to embellish with tiny glass marbles. Apply clear crystal lacquer to these areas and sprinkle with marbles. Gently tap off excess.

2 Apply a coat of clear crystal lacquer to the remaining areas of each design. Allow to dry thoroughly.

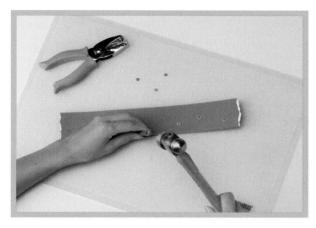

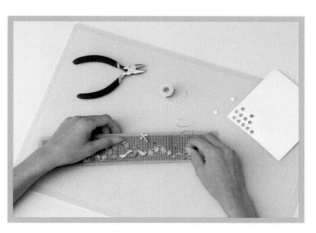

3 Cut a 2" blue strip for the border and a 5½ x 3½" rectangle for the title. Trim and apply self-adhesive screen. Randomly punch holes for eyelets. To set each eyelet, insert an eyelet on the mesh side and turn over to the backside. Insert an eyelet setter into the eyelet tube and tap several times with a small hammer. Turn back to the front side, cover eyelet with a soft cloth, and tap again with a hammer. Repeat until all eyelets are set.

4 Cut a length of thin craft wire twice the length of the border or title. Randomly lace the wire in and out of the eyelets as desired. Curve and loop the wire between eyelets. Secure the wire ends beneath an embellishment or tape to the back of the title or border.

MATERIALS

- One sheet each of white, yellow, green and periwinkle solid-colored paper
- Bugs paper punch-outs (Creative Imaginations)
- Clear crystal lacquer (Sakura Hobby Craft)
- Clear Micro Beedz (Art Accents)
- Self-adhesive mesh screen (Magic Mesh by Avant 'Card)
- ⅛" hole punch
- Colored eyelets (Impress Rubber Stamps)
- Eyelet setter
- Small hammer
- Thin craft wire (Artistic Wire)
- Self-adhesive foam spacers

Fancy Vegetables
EMBELLISH PAPER PIECINGS

Jodi Amidei, Lafayette, Colorado
Inspired by Dana Swords, Fredericksburg, Virginia

The next time you're at the craft store, pick up a few decorative items such as glitter, beads, fiber, sequins, squiggle eyes, doll hair, confetti, yarn and embroidery floss. These items come in handy when you want to add sparkle and texture to die cuts, punched shapes, template shapes, printed designs or any page element. For this garden page background, mat a trimmed sheet of light green paper with dark green. Create the embellished vegetables as shown on the facing page. For the title, mat a 6¾ x 1¾" patterned rectangle with green; adhere carrots for each letter part; complete each letter with green pen. Crop and mat photos with cream, green and patterned paper. For the left photo, accent punched and folded cream photo corners with carrots. Print and mat caption. For the border, mat a 3" patterned strip with green, tearing one long edge of each piece. Arrange vegetables on border using self-adhesive foam spacers as desired.

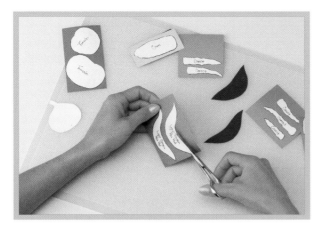

1 Use the vegetable patterns to cut out each vegetable piece from various solid-colored papers.

2 Shade each piece with colored chalk and draw details with black pen.

3 Use liquid adhesive to embellish vegetables with color-coordinated sequins, seed beads, glitter and tiny glass marbles.

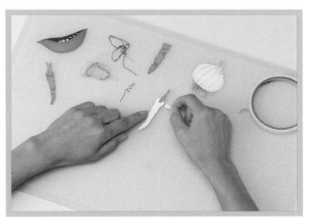

4 Tape strands of green embroidery floss to the back of the carrots. Accent onion with tan fiber. Tape spiraled lengths of green craft wire beneath the ends of the string beans.

MATERIALS

- Vegetable patterns on page 90
- One sheet each of green, light green and cream solid-colored paper
- One sheet leaf patterned paper (Keeping Memories Alive)
- Scraps of orange, red and yellow solid-colored paper for vegetables
- Colored chalk
- Black and green pens
- Orange seed beads (Westrim)
- Green sequins (Westrim)
- Red Micro Beedz (Art Accents)
- Yellow glitter (Magic Scraps)
- Green embroidery floss
- Funky Fibers™ (Lily Lake Crafts) for onion
- Green craft wire (Artistic Wire)
- Corner pocket punch (Marvy/Uchida)
- Self-adhesive foam spacer

Tied Tags
CONNECT DESIGNS WITH COLORFUL FIBER

Marpy Hayse, Katy, Texas

Use any kind of fiber or paper strips to tie together similar elements such as journaling blocks, stamped designs, stickers, die cuts, punch art or even vintage color clip art. To create the seed-packet border, follow the steps on the facing page. Mount border on left side of rust patterned background. Crop photo and mat with sage. Stamp and embellish cream mat and small tags using the same technique as for the large tags. Cut 7 x 2½" sage strip for the title; wrap fiber around right side; layer over ⅜" sage strips; adhere letter stickers. Stamp and cut out angel; shade with colored pencils. Mount angel and small tags using self-adhesive foam spacers. Mount seed label beneath vellum tag and arrange below title.

1 Stamp tags using decorative stamp and brown stamping ink.

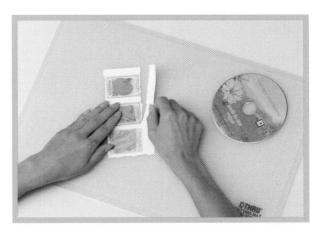

2 Print CD-ROM seed-packet graphics sized to fit on the tags. Tear along the edges of each seed packet.

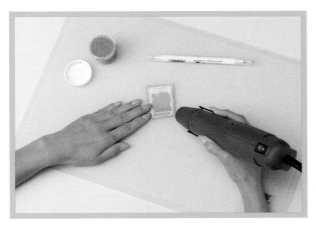

3 Emboss torn edges of seed packets using an embossing pen, embossing powder and a heat gun. Mount packets on tags. For the eyelets, punch a ⅛" hole in the center of a small punched circle. Insert copper eyelet through circle and then through tag. Set eyelet. Repeat for each tag.

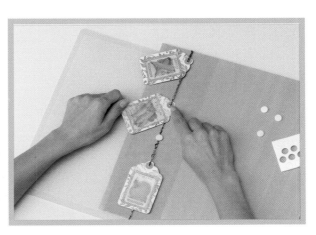

4 String tags onto fiber. Mount vertically on a 3½ x 12" sage strip using self-adhesive foam spacers. Tape fiber ends to back of border strip.

VARIATION

Stamped, colored and torn seashell designs are united in this beach theme with cream-colored paper raffia. (Paper and letter stickers by Creative Imaginations, stamps by Hero Arts)

Marpy Hayse, Katy, Texas

Intaglio Shrink Art
WATCH THE MAGIC OF INCREDIBLY SHRINKING PLASTIC

Pam Hornschu for Stampendous

Shrink plastic is just plain fun. You just never get tired of watching a thin sheet of plastic shrink into a design half the size and more than twice as thick. And the design possibilities are limitless. For this zoo page, first stamp brown cheetah spots on a 9½" tan ribbed square. Crop photos and mat with pumpkin paper. Print caption on brown vellum; tear edges as well as orange and cream vellum accents. Punch ⅛" holes and adhere eyelet stickers. For the background, stamp black zebra stripes around edges of 11½" brown square; punch two ¼" holes in upper left and upper right corners. Tie together pieces of natural raffia, tying ends through punched holes. Mount tan square on brown square; mat with black background sheet. Create the shrink plastic letters as shown on the facing page. Tie each letter to the raffia with black twine and mount with self-adhesive foam spacers. To create the corner accents, stamp triangles of ivory shrink plastic; shrink and cool, flattening with the back of a stamp.

MATERIALS

- One sheet tan, ribbed solid-colored paper
- One sheet each of black, brown and pumpkin solid-colored paper
- One sheet each of orange, cream and brown vellum paper
- Zebra Stripes, Cheetah Spots, Prancing Zebra, Giraffes and Kenya Montage stamps (Stampendous)
- Black, brown, orange and white stamping inks (Stampendous)
- Class A' Peel eyelet stickers (Stampendous)
- Natural raffia
- Lettering template (Provo Craft)
- Black and ivory shrink plastic (K & B Innovations)
- Stabilo pencil
- ¼" and ⅛" hole punch
- Talcum powder
- Black twine
- Self-adhesive foam spacers

1 Trace letters from template onto scrap paper. Use a photocopy machine to enlarge letters about twice the size, keeping in mind that the letters will shrink to nearly one-half their original size when heated. Trace letters onto shrink plastic with a Stabilo pencil and cut out.

2 Punch ¼" holes at the top of each letter. Dust the front and back of each letter with talcum powder to prevent sticking during shrinkage. Before shrinking each letter, ink the stamp you want to use in Step 3. One at a time, heat each letter with an embossing gun for about 30 seconds, holding it down with an embossing stylus or other heat-safe tool. The letter will curl during heating and flatten when shrinkage is complete.

3 While the letter is still warm, immediately press an inked stamp into the shrunken plastic to reverse-emboss the image, creating an "intaglio" or carved look.

4 When the stamped letter images have dried and cooled, accent each letter by brushing it with another ink color.

VARIATION

Experiment with shrink plastic silhouette shapes (Stampendous) to create shaped and curved seashells and sea glass that look amazingly realistic. (Stamps by Stampendous on frost shrink plastic, shell stickers by Stampendous)

Pam Hornschu for Stampendous

Knotted Twine
STRING BUTTONS AND PUNCHED SHAPES

Jenna Beegle, Woodstock, Georgia

If you can tie a knot, you can easily assemble these star and heart designs. Vary the look by changing the embellishments. For example, connect hearts with pink thread for Valentine's Day, or tie balloons to a bow for a birthday theme. For this all-American page, write the title and caption with a blue pen on 1½" cream strips; shade edges with brown chalk; mat title with navy. Triple mat photo with navy, cream and burgundy. Create frayed fabric border and heart and star accents as shown on the facing page; layer with page elements on tan background.

1 Trim star printed fabric to 2½ x 11½" rectangle and fray edges. Use a Xyron machine or double-sided sheet adhesive to apply adhesive to the back of the fabric.

2 Use star pattern to cut out two burgundy stars. Punch primitive hearts and stars. Shade star edges with brown chalk. Draw heart and star details with black pen.

3 Punch a ⅛" hole in the center of each large star. For each star, insert a silver eyelet through the hole from the front, turn over, insert eyelet setter, and tap with a hammer. Turn to the front and tap eyelet again.

4 Thread several strands of thin white twine through each eyelet. Tie a knot on top of each star to connect the strands and prevent them from slipping through the eyelet. Punch ¹⁄₁₆" holes in the centers of the small hearts and stars. String loose ends of twine through punched shapes and buttons. Secure ends with slipknots.

MATERIALS

- Star pattern on page 91
- One sheet each of tan, burgundy, navy and cream solid-colored paper
- Navy and black pens
- Brown chalk
- Strip of star printed fabric (source unknown)
- Medium primitive star and heart and super jumbo primitive heart punches (Emagination Crafts)
- ⅛" and ¹⁄₁₆" hole punches
- Silver eyelets (Impress Rubber Stamps)
- Thin white twine or embroidery floss
- Two- and four-hole buttons

Twisted Wire
COIL AND SPIRAL COPPER WIRE

Torrey Miller, Westminster, Colorado

Craft wire is a blast. With just wire cutters and pliers you can bend, coil, twist and crimp all sorts of artistic embellishments and fasteners to hold memorabilia or photos. For this travel page, trim a sheet of pumpkin paper for the background and mat with black. Mount sheet of textured paper. Trim and punch 1¼" black strip for belt. Print caption; cut into tag shape and punch hole. Cut and punch an additional blank tag. Shade caption, blank tag and tag die cuts with brown chalk. Write year on round tag. Create and attach wire holders as shown on the facing page. Use a similar technique to bend and attach wire letters and tag accents. Adhere poster stickers to scrap paper; trim ends with stamp scissors. Mount poster stickers and photos by slipping between wire coils and mounting to page with self-adhesive foam spacers.

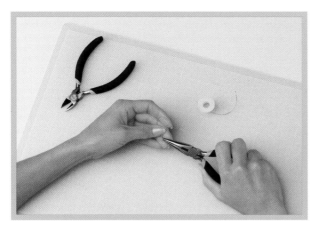

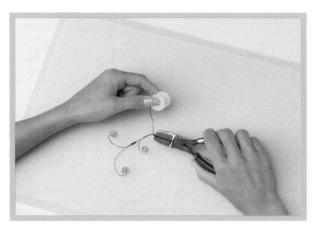

1 For each wire holder, start with a long piece of wire for the base. Cut several 3 to 4" lengths of wire for the "branches." Curl one end of each piece into a round, square or triangular flat coil. For the round coils, curl wire around the tip of round-nose jewelry pliers or a thin round object such as a nail or toothpick. For the square or triangular coils, use flat pliers to bend each wire corner.

2 Take the uncoiled end of each piece of wire and wrap it tightly around the base wire. Trim ends with wire cutters. Repeat for each coil. To keep the coils from sliding up and down the base wire, put cloth between a pair of flat pliers and pinch each coil firmly.

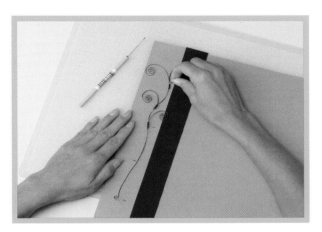

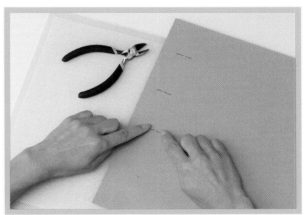

3 To attach wire holder to the background, place it in the desired position. Use a needle or straight pin to punch pairs of holes on each side of the wire. Cut 1" lengths of wire and fold in half to form U-shaped fasteners. Insert fastener ends over wire piece into two holes. Repeat for each fastener.

4 Turn page over and press fastener ends flat. Cover ends with tape.

MATERIALS

- One sheet each of tan and mustard solid-colored paper
- One sheet plus one strip black textured paper (Bazzill)
- One sheet faux reptile skin textured paper (source unknown)
- Tag die cuts (DMD Industries)
- 24-gauge copper craft wire (The Beadery)
- Wire cutters and round pliers
- Travel poster stickers (Stampa Rosa)
- Stamp decorative scissors (Fiskars)
- ¼" hole punch
- Self-adhesive foam spacers
- Brown pen

String-Tie Brad Fasteners
WIND UP A FOLDOUT BORDER

Kelly Angard, Highlands Ranch, Colorado

Re-create the string and button closure of "interdepartmental" business envelopes with a string-tie fastener for a simple foldout border. It's a fun look that also increases your page real estate. For the background, mat a trimmed sheet of olive paper with brown strips. Create the foldout border as shown on the facing page. Tear the long edge of a 5" strip of stamp patterned paper; mount at page bottom. For the pocket, mount cut and torn brown strips around the edges of an 8¼ x 5" cream vellum rectangle; adhere to page along left, bottom and right edges. Create brad fasteners for pocket using the same technique as for the foldout border. Crop and mat photos and printed captions; slip into pocket.

MATERIALS

- Fold-out pattern on page 91
- One sheet each of olive, dark olive, tan and brown solid-colored paper
- One sheet marble patterned paper (Scrap Ease)
- One sheet postage stamp patterned paper (Anna Griffin)
- One sheet cream vellum
- Lettering template (EK Success)
- Letter stickers (Creative Memories)
- Vintage Travel printed page accents (Fresh Cuts by EK Success)
- Brass brad fasteners (Creative Trends)
- Silver to Black jewelry oxidizer (source unknown)
- Cream cotton string (Making Memories) or embroidery floss
- Gold photo corners (Canson)

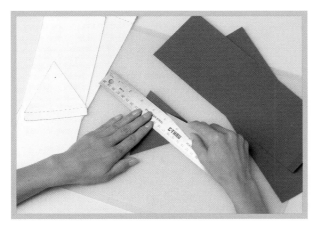

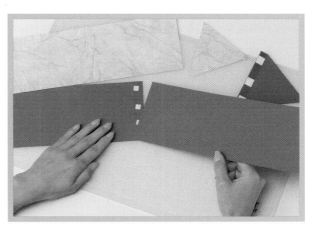

1 Transfer foldout patterns to brown paper and cut out. Use a metal ruler and bone folder to score and fold along the fold lines on the triangular and one rectangular piece.

2 Assemble the foldout border by mounting the remaining rectangular piece over the folded tabs of the other two pieces. Close the foldout border and adhere marble patterned paper to the fronts of the front flap and the triangle.

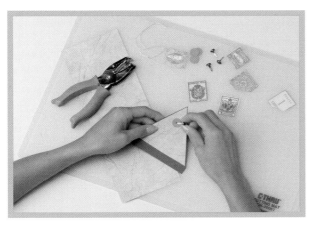

3 Embellish the front flaps with dark olive title letters, printed page accents and stamps cut from patterned paper. Prepare each brad fastener by dipping it in a jewelry oxidizer to give it an antique look. For each brad fastener, punch a ¼" small tan circle. Punch a ¼" hole in the center of each circle. Punch holes in the front flaps where you want to fasten each brad. Attach each brad through a punched circle and hole, flattening the ends on the back and taping down if necessary. Cut lengths of string and tie ends in a slipknot; wind around brad fasteners beneath punched circles.

4 Open the foldout border. Trim and mat photos; mount with gold photo corners.

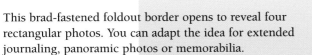

This brad-fastened foldout border opens to reveal four rectangular photos. You can adapt the idea for extended journaling, panoramic photos or memorabilia.

Layered Scenes
TEAR SAND, WATER, HILLS AND SKY

Beth Rogers, Mesa, Arizona

This quick and easy idea makes a huge design impact. Change the scene to fit the venue, whether snowy hills, mountains and trees, streams and rivers or gorgeous sunsets. For this beach theme, start with a tan background. Tear blue and navy strips to layer beneath title letters. Create title letters and border as shown on the facing page. Write remaining title words with silver metallic pen. Crop and mat photos. Use similar tearing and layering technique to create photo corner accents. Print caption on white vellum paper; layer over photo and blue mat.

MATERIALS

- One sheet each of tan, navy and blue solid-colored paper
- One sheet each of blue, light blue and white vellum paper
- One sheet each of cloud (Hot Off The Press) and sand (Sandylion) patterned paper
- Block Upper lettering template (EK Success)
- Jumbo and super jumbo square punches (Marvy/Uchida)
- Silver metallic pen

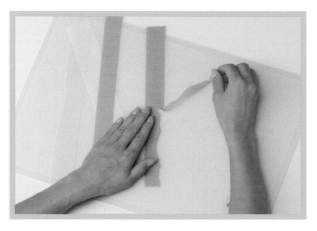

1 Cut several 11 x 1½" strips of vellum and sand patterned paper. Tear long edges of each strip.

2 Cut two 11 x 1½" strips of cloud patterned paper, one for the border and one for the title letters. Layer, overlap and adhere torn strips atop cloud strips to create scene.

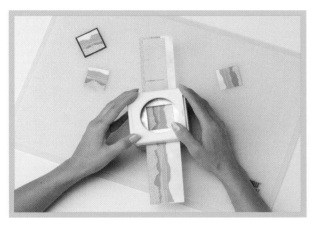

3 Insert border strip face up into upside-down jumbo square punch. Punch squares from border with minimal waste between squares. Punch super jumbo navy squares to mat each square.

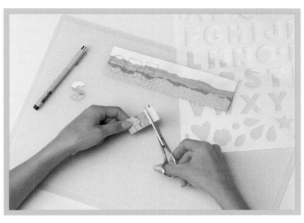

4 Use template to trace letters onto second border strip. Cut out each letter using a craft knife and cutting mat.

VARIATION

Recall camping fun by punching tiny trees and layering with torn brown hills. Match the colors to the photos. (Tree punch by McGill)

Beth Rogers, Mesa, Arizona

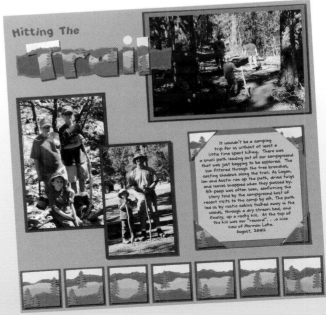

Embellished Edges
TEXTURIZE TORN STRIPS

Brandi Ginn, Lafayette, Colorado
Inspired by Kathleen Aho, Rochester, Minnesota

The fancy edges in this beach scene not only add sparkle and texture but also mimic the high tide line at the beach. Pull colors from your photos to embellish torn edges to match your page theme. For this project, start with a light blue background. Tear and embellish strips for border following the steps on the facing page. Layer strips at page bottom. Crop and mat photos. Tear and embellish strips for the page title and photo corner accents using a similar technique, however cut out the title letters before embellishing. Write remaining title words with black pen on tan strips. Print caption. Accent border with tiny seashells and starfish.

MATERIALS

- One sheet each of blue, light blue, tan and light tan solid-colored paper
- One sheet each of light blue and dark blue patterned paper (Paper Adventures, Magenta)
- Copper embossing powder (Stampin' Up)
- Silver Micro Beedz (Art Accents)
- Blue glitter (Art Institute Glitter)
- Clear/silver seed beads (Westrim)
- Glitter glue
- Liquid adhesive
- Tiny seashells and starfish (Magic Scraps, U.S. Shell)
- Black pen

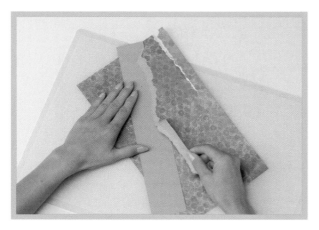

1 Tear top edges of solid and patterned strips for the border.

2 To emboss a torn edge, brush with an embossing pen, sprinkle with embossing powder, and remove excess. Heat with an embossing gun until set.

3 To embellish with tiny glass marbles, seed beads or glitter, apply liquid adhesive to torn edges. Use a generous amount of adhesive for beads. For glitter, use glitter glue, which spreads more evenly and allows the glitter to adhere without clumping. Sprinkle glued areas with embellishment and press lightly with fingertips. Gently shake off any excess.

VARIATION

Monochromatic embellishments add further elegance to this torn-edge technique. (Shaved Ice glitter by Magic Scraps)

Brandi Ginn, Lafayette, Colorado
Photos Brian Cummings, Aliso Creek, California

Fall

The leaves dance in the crisp air while pumpkins smile their silly jack-o-lantern grins and the aroma of roasted turkey wafts through the house. There's much to be thankful for with these handmade page notions and ideas!

• Vellum pockets • Stamped leaves • Lacquered stamping • Metallic leafing
• Tab-top curtains • Fancy gift bags • Paper cord mosaic • Border collage
• Aged tag art

There you have it: a year-round smorgasbord of delightful scrapbooking techniques that you can apply to any scrapbook page—regardless of its theme!

Vellum Pockets
STITCH BEADED CORNERS

Brandi Ginn, Lafayette, Colorado

Pressed flowers, punched snowflakes, movie ticket stubs and postage stamps are just a few of the things you can put in these vellum pockets. For this leafy version, start with a patterned background. For the title, stamp brown letters on tan paper and color letters with gold pen. Cut out each word; brush edges with brown ink; mat with rust paper. Mount title over fiber using self-adhesive foam spacers. Create the border as shown on the facing page. Mat photos with sage paper. Embellish photo corners in the same manner as the lower corners of the vellum pockets. Print caption; tear edges and color with brown ink; attach with mini brad fasteners.

1 Cut a 2½" sage strip and five 1¾ x 1" vellum rectangles. Adhere the first leaf sticker at the top of the border. Holding a vellum rectangle in place over the sticker, use an awl or straight pin to pierce four holes at each lower corner—two holes on the side and two holes on the bottom to form an asymmetrical X. Pierce two holes near each upper corner. Pierce through both the vellum and the sage background. Repeat this step for each leaf sticker and vellum rectangle. Pierce two additional sets of holes at the bottom of the border for the wire accent.

2 Thread three strands of embroidery floss on a beading needle and knot ends together. Stitch Xs across the vellum pocket corners, stringing three seed beads onto the top stitch of each X. Stitch the upper corners, stringing one bead onto each stitch. Secure loose ends to the back of the border. String seed beads onto a short length of craft wire; slip ends through pierced holes at the bottom of the border; curl ends. Mat border with rust paper; tear edges.

MATERIALS

- One sheet stripe patterned paper (Frances Meyer)
- One sheet each of rust, sage and tan solid-colored paper
- One sheet white vellum
- Letter stamps (Stampin' Up)
- Brown stamping ink (Colorbök)
- Gold metallic pen
- Adornaments fiber (K1C2)
- Self-adhesive foam spacers
- Leaf stickers (Stickopotamus)
- Awl or straight pin
- Beading needle
- Brown embroidery floss (DMC)
- Seed beads (Magic Scraps)
- Gold-colored craft wire (Darice)
- Mini brad fasteners (HyGlo/AmericanPin)

Stamped Leaves

AIR-BRUSH AN AUTUMN THEME

Terri Davenport, Toledo, Ohio

A spray bulb ink applicator is just one way to texturize a solid-colored background. You can "faux finish" any page element to add texture, depth and dimension. Try sponge painting, chalking, watercolors, or adding stripes or polka dots. Find inspiration in the patterns and theme of the photos. For this autumn page, create the border, title background and leaf accents following the steps on the facing page. Use a similar technique to splatter, stamp and wrap the title letters. Print and trim caption; splatter with ink. Mat photos and caption with rust paper.

1 Cut 2¾" tan strips for the title and border and 2" tan strips for the smaller leaf accents. Insert a brush pen into a spray bulb applicator and splatter tan strips with various colors.

2 Randomly stamp leaves using brown and green stamping ink. Stamp off the edges of the title and border strips. Stamp a leaf in the center of each smaller strip. When you are finished stamping, mat each strip with rust paper.

3 Wrap border with jute. Use a craft knife to cut slits in the smaller leaf accents; wrap jute through slits and around edge. Secure all loose ends to the backside of each piece.

MATERIALS

- One sheet each of tan and rust solid-colored paper
- Inkworkx spray bulb applicator (EK Success)
- Brush-tip colored pens
- Leaf and letter stamps (Stampin' Up)
- Green and brown stamping inks
- Jute

Lacquered Stamping
CREATE GLOSSY, DIMENSIONAL IMAGES

MaryJo Regier, Littleton, Colorado
Inspired by Jan Monahan, Dayton, Ohio

Color crystal lacquer adds a subtle hint of dimension to stamped images, stickers and pre-printed die cuts or punch outs. Embossing before lacquering raises the image just enough to "corral" the paint. You can also color theme clip art by first tracing with an embossing pen and then embossing with powder. For the background, trim a sheet of cream paper and mat with orange. Mount a 10½" evergreen square at an angle on the background. Print words for title and caption mat on cream paper. Trim title to 2¼" strip and caption to 7 x 4½" rectangle. Mount photo over caption mat. Wrap raffia strips around ends of title strip and left edge and right corner of page; secure loose ends to the back with tape. Follow the steps on the facing page to stamp, lacquer and cut out pumpkins. Use a similar technique to create title letters. Mount pumpkins and letters with self-adhesive foam spacers, tucking edges beneath raffia as desired.

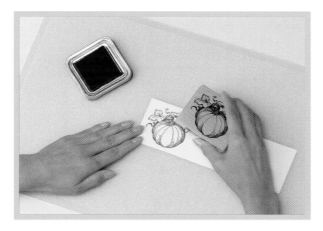

1 Stamp pumpkins on cream paper with embossing ink.

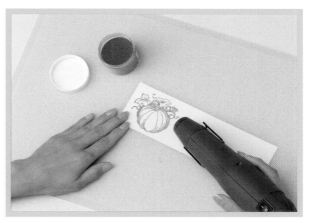

2 Sprinkle each image with gold embossing powder and tap off excess. Heat with an embossing gun to set powder.

3 Color image with 3-D color crystal lacquer, shading as desired. For added dimension, let the first coat dry and then apply a second coat. Allow each coat to dry at least 30 minutes.

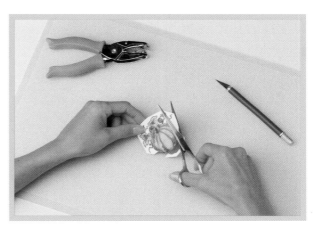

4 Silhouette-crop each stamped image. Use a craft knife to cut around vines and a small hole punch to cut holes in vines.

MATERIALS

- One to two sheets each of orange, cream and evergreen solid-colored paper
- Natural raffia
- Pumpkin stamp (PSX Design)
- Letter stamps (Close To My Heart)
- Embossing ink pad
- Gold embossing powder
- Embossing heat gun
- Small hole punch
- 3-D colored crystal lacquer (Sakura Hobby Craft)
- Self-adhesive foam spacers

Metallic Leafing
GILD STAMPED IMAGES

Jodi Amidei, Lafayette, Colorado

MATERIALS

- One to two sheets each of black, rust and cranberry solid-colored paper
- Leaf stamp (Stampin' Up)
- Embossing ink pad
- Heat & Stick powder adhesive (Biblical Impressions)
- Variegated metallic leafing (Biblical Impressions)
- ⅛" Terrifically Tacky tape adhesive (Art Accents)
- Lettering templates (Wordsworth)
- Glue pen (Ek Success)
- Corner pocket punch (Marvy/uchida)

Metallic leafing is available in a variety of colors, so you can easily find colors to coordinate with any theme. Start with a black background. Create the border and title as described on the facing page. Crop and double mat photos with cream and rust paper. Punch and fold black photo corners. Use tape adhesive to embellish photo corners with metallic leaf. Cut an additional cranberry mat for the photo with corners. Print and double mat caption. Stamp, gild and cut out an additional leaf; mount with self-adhesive foam spacers.

1 Stamp leaves with clear embossing ink on black paper. Sprinkle powder adhesive over the image and shake off excess. Heat with embossing gun until image becomes shiny and tacky. Do not overheat.

2 Use a medium stiff brush to apply metallic leaf until image is completely covered. Brush off excess.

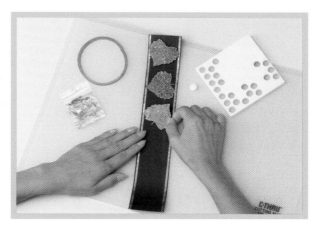

3 Gently buff each image with a soft cloth or old sock to polish and remove loose flakes.

4 Cut a 2" black strip for the border. Apply tape adhesive to both long edges. Apply metallic leaf in the same manner as Steps 2 and 3. Mount gilded leaves on border strip using self-adhesive foam spacers for every other leaf.

5 For the title, trace the first letter using a lettering template and glue pen. Let the glue dry to a tacky stage and then apply metallic leaf as described in Steps 2 and 3. Repeat for each remaining letter. Trim title and mat with rust paper.

Tab-Top Curtains
BUTTON DOWN PAPER FLAPS

Torrey Miller, Westminster, Colorado
Photos Tracy Johnson, Thornton, Colorado; MaryJo Regier, Littleton, Colorado

This whimsical design, based on the popular curtain style, can also be embellished with beads, flowers, tassels, snaps, eyelets, ribbons and bows—whatever best suits your page theme. For this button version, trim and mat a patterned sheet for the background. Write title word at top left corner. Follow the steps on the facing page to create the tab-top section. For the title, cut evergreen letters using template. Double mat each letter with punched squares, mounting every other letter at an angle; draw letter highlights in white ink. To form hanging loops for each letter, punch two holes and thread ends of a 6" piece of yarn through each hole from the back. "Hang" letters over buttons and mount on background; tie knots and trim yarn ends. Mat photos with cream. Trim opposite corners of turkey photo; mat again; fold corners; adhere buttons; mat again. Print and mat caption.

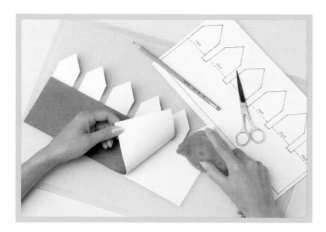

1 Transfer tab-top pattern to the back of evergreen patterned paper and cut out. Mount a 3" evergreen strip over the lower part of the tab section on the wrong side.

2 Mount a second 11½ x 9½" sage patterned square so that it covers all but about ¾" of the evergreen strip. Mount a ⅜" wood-grain patterned strip at the top of the evergreen strip with self-adhesive foam spacers. Bend tabs down over dowel and adhere points to sage patterned square.

MATERIALS

- Tab-top pattern on page 92
- One sheet each of cream, sage, evergreen and dark evergreen solid-colored paper
- One to two sheets each of sage and evergreen patterned paper (Anna Griffin)
- One ⅜" strip of wood-grain patterned paper (Frances Meyer)
- Green pen
- Self-adhesive foam spacers
- Buttons
- Glue dots (Glue Dots, Int'l)
- Lettering template (Scrap Pagerz)
- Square punches (EK Success, Marvy/Uchida)
- ⅛" hole punch
- Yarn

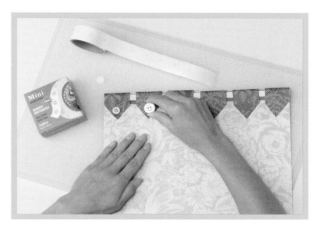

3 Mount buttons over tabs with glue dots.

VARIATION

For a softer, "less dimensional" version of the tab-top design, select coordinating shades of solid, printed (Doodlebug Design) and vellum (Paper Adventures) papers. Attach the tabs and folded photo corners with white flower and lavender eyelets (Making Memories).

Torrey Miller, Westminster, Colorado
Photo Pam Klassen, Westminster, Colorado

Fancy Gift Bags

WRAP UP YOUR HOLIDAY SHOPPING

Nicole Hinrichs Ramsaroop
Horst, The Netherlands

MATERIALS

- Bag pattern on page 92
- Several sheets of various shades of brown solid-colored paper
- One sheet of pearl white Bravissimo paper (Emagination Crafts)
- One sheet brown corrugated paper (DMD)
- One sheet white mulberry paper (PrintWorks)
- Gold foil tissue paper
- ⅛" hole punch
- Natural and brown Twistel paper raffia (Making Memories)
- Fiber
- Brown stamping ink

You can adapt these holiday bags for any gift-giving occasion from birthdays and anniversaries to weddings and baby showers. Create the gift bags as shown on the facing page. Mount two bags on a 3½" matted strip of brown corrugated paper. Mount border on left side of brown background. Cut 4" brown corrugated square in half for lower right corner; mount last shopping bag over triangle. Cut title letters using computer font as template; layer with fiber and untwisted paper raffia on brown rectangle; tear edges; double mat with white and gold foil tissue. Print and mat caption. Crop and arrange photos. Color bag and photo labels as shown on the facing page; use the same technique to color handwritten date for title. Mat labels with brown paper or white mulberry.

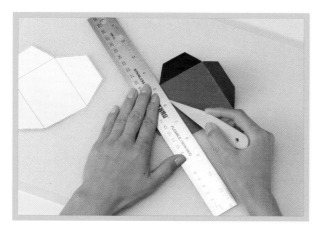

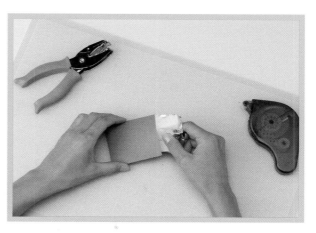

1 Use bag pattern to cut out three brown bags. Before folding bags, use a metal edge ruler and a bone folder or embossing stylus to score along fold lines.

2 Punch small holes at the upper edge of each bag for the handles. Gather and crumple together two 3" foil and mulberry squares; tuck inside bag. Secure on the backside with tape.

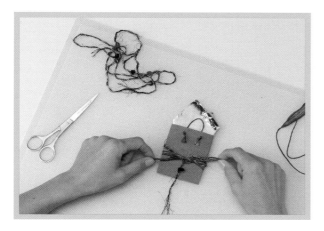

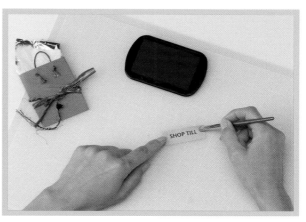

3 For the handle, insert ends of untwisted paper raffia into punched holes; tie knots and trim ends. Combine lengths of untwisted paper raffia with fiber; tie around bag and knot on the front side; trim ends.

4 Print labels for bags and photos and cut out. Use a small stiff brush and brown stamping ink to stipple color onto each tag with an up and down pouncing motion.

VARIATION

Four birthday candles light up this colorful birthday page. Torn pieces of colored and patterned paper and chunky, textured fiber lend a festive look to the gift bags.

Nicole Hinrichs Ramsaroop, Horst, The Netherlands

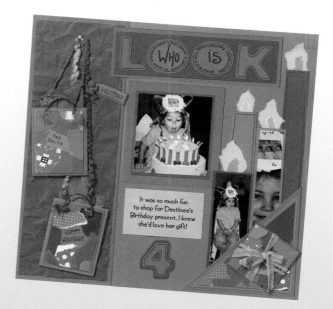

Paper Cord Mosaic
REARRANGE STAMPED AND PATTERNED STRIPS

Tricia Morris for Club Scrap

These mosaics are simply gorgeous and the colors can be changed to fit any page theme. You build them using strips of paper rather than cutting and arranging tiny squares. Follow the steps on the facing page to learn the technique. For the background, use eyelets to attach an 8½" square of patterned vellum diagonally to a sheet of mustard paper. For the corners, cut mosaics into triangles and double mat long edges. For the photo, cut another mosaic strip in half and double mat outside edges. Arrange strips above and below photo on mustard and brown mats. Cut, stamp and mat large tag; adhere eyelet and fiber; write caption; mat with mosaic strip and brown paper. Write captions on mini tags; shade with yellow ink; adhere with mini brad fasteners and self-adhesive foam spacers. Sew beads to shaded yellow scrap; write year.

1 Randomly stamp solid-colored paper to create custom designs. Choose coordinating patterned papers. Cut stamped and patterned paper strips at least 2½" wide at random angles.

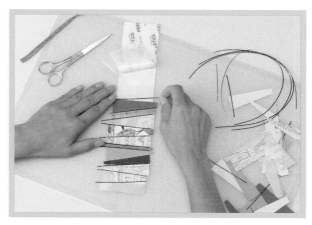

2 Cut a strip of double-sided tape at least 2" wide. Remove one side of the backing and lay on a flat surface, sticky side up. Starting at one end of the tape strip, adhere a paper strip, then a piece of paper cord, then a different paper strip. Continue this process until the tape strip is covered.

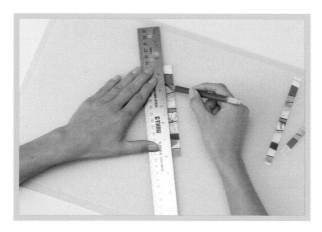

3 Using a metal edge ruler and a craft knife, trim excess paper and cord from both edges of the tape. Then cut the border into long strips approximately ½" wide.

4 Alternate the direction of every other strip so that the colors are rearranged and produce a mosaic effect. Mount the cut strips on another piece of double-sided tape, alternating strips with lengths of paper cord, trimming as needed. Mat each completed design.

MATERIALS

• One sheet each of mustard, light brown and dark brown solid-colored paper (Club Scrap)

• One sheet patterned vellum (Club Scrap)

• Coordinating solid and patterned papers for mosaic

• Miscellaneous stamps and stamping ink for mosaic

• Various colors of Mizuhiki paper cord (Yasutomo and Company)

• Gold-colored eyelets (Making Memories)

• Fiber

• Black pen

• Mini tags

• Mini brad fasteners (Creative Impressions)

• Letter and amber beads (Westrim)

• Self-adhesive foam spacers

Border Collage
BLEND PHOTOS AND MEMORABILIA

Pam Klassen, Westminster, Colorado
Tree by David Cobb, Thornton, Colorado

MATERIALS

- Tree pattern on page 92
- One sheet each of cream and black solid-colored paper
- Black pen
- Colored chalk
- Color-copied photos, memorabilia, pressed flowers, etc. for collage
- Skeletonized leaves (All Night Media)
- Lettering template (Wordsworth)

The collage technique is a great way to use up extra photos and memorabilia from any occasion. Layer Christmas cards, ticket stubs, airline tickets, birthday confetti or whatever elements fit the theme. For the family tree design, use the pattern to trace the tree onto cream background paper. Outline tree and write names with black pen. Shade tree and background with colored chalk. Create the top and right collage borders as shown on the facing page. To mount the title, trim around the uppermost leaves on the tree through the background paper; slip title border beneath leaves and mount on top edge of page. Write caption on cream strip and mat with brown.

1 Gather collage elements such as color photocopies of heritage photos, memorabilia, skeletonized leaves, pressed flowers and ribbon. Collect enough material for two collages—one for the side border and one for the title.

2 Arrange and layer items as desired to form collage on right side. Mount items and trim edges as necessary.

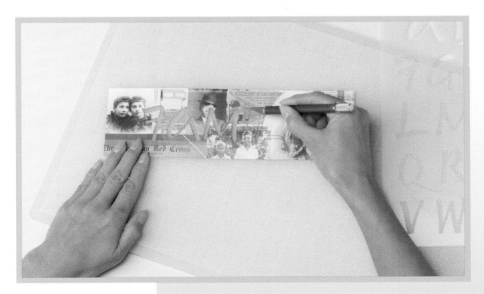

3 For the title, arrange and mount a second collage on a 3" strip of paper, trimming edges as necessary. Use template to pencil letter outlines on collage. Using a craft knife and cutting mat, cut out each letter through all layers. Mount a 2" black strip beneath the letter openings.

Aged Tag Art
SHADE WITH COLORED CHALK

Betsy Bell Sammarco, New Canaan, Connecticut

MATERIALS

- Tag pattern on page 92
- One sheet green patterned paper (Anna Griffin)
- One sheet each of cream, lavender, sage and brown solid-colored paper
- ¾" square punch
- ¼" and ⅛" hole punches
- Black brush pen and journaling pens
- Colored chalk
- Floral stickers (Debbie Mumm)
- Cream embroidery floss (DMC)

This simple aging technique works well not only for heritage photos but also for outdoor, western and masculine themes. Add the technique to any layout for a vintage or old-fashioned effect. Create and "age" tags for title as shown on the facing page. Wrap lengths of cream embroidery floss through each tag hole and tie bows. Mount tags at top of green patterned background. Use the same technique to create and age narrow ¾" tags for the border, cutting small brown rectangles and punching ⅛" holes at each end; tie together with embroidery floss. Write and age caption; adhere flower sticker. Crop and mat photos, using an aged mat for right photo. Cut out and age cream corner accents and adhere stickers.

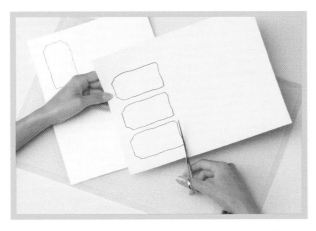

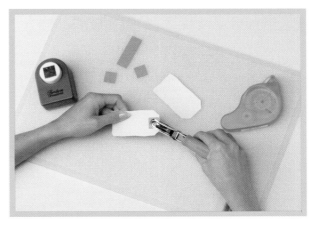

1 Use pattern to trace tags onto cream paper. Cut out tags.

2 Punch ¾" brown squares and adhere to top of each tag. Punch ¼" holes through the center of each square.

3 Color tag edges with black brush pen. Shade edges with brown chalk. Adhere stickers.

VARIATION

Shade stamped tags (stamps by Stampin' Up) with brightly colored chalk for a contemporary take on the aging technique. The torn edges on the patterned border background (All My Memories) are slightly curled up for added texture.

Brandi Ginn, Lafayette, Colorado

Project Patterns

Use these reproducible project patterns to complete scrapbook pages featured in this book. Enlarge patterns on a photocopier by the percentage shown. When transferring patterns to your paper of choice, be sure to note solid, continuous lines for cut lines and dotted lines for fold lines.

Row houses, pages 4-5, 93 (200%)

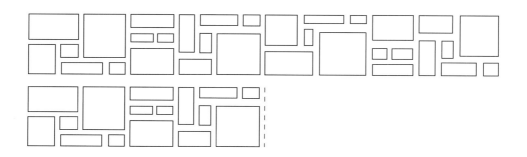

Vellum stained glass, page 24 (200%)

COOKIES

Frosted letters, page 26 (200%)

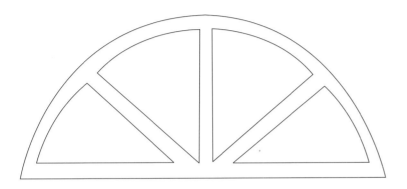

Window shaker box, page 16 (200%)

Peek-a-boo window, page 20 (200%)

Threaded accents, pages 28 (200%)

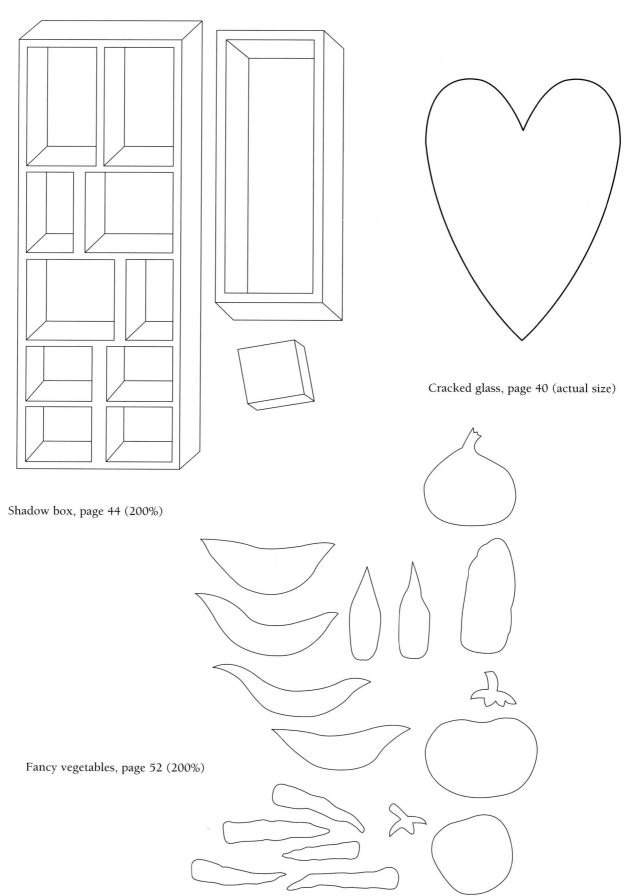

Cracked glass, page 40 (actual size)

Shadow box, page 44 (200%)

Fancy vegetables, page 52 (200%)

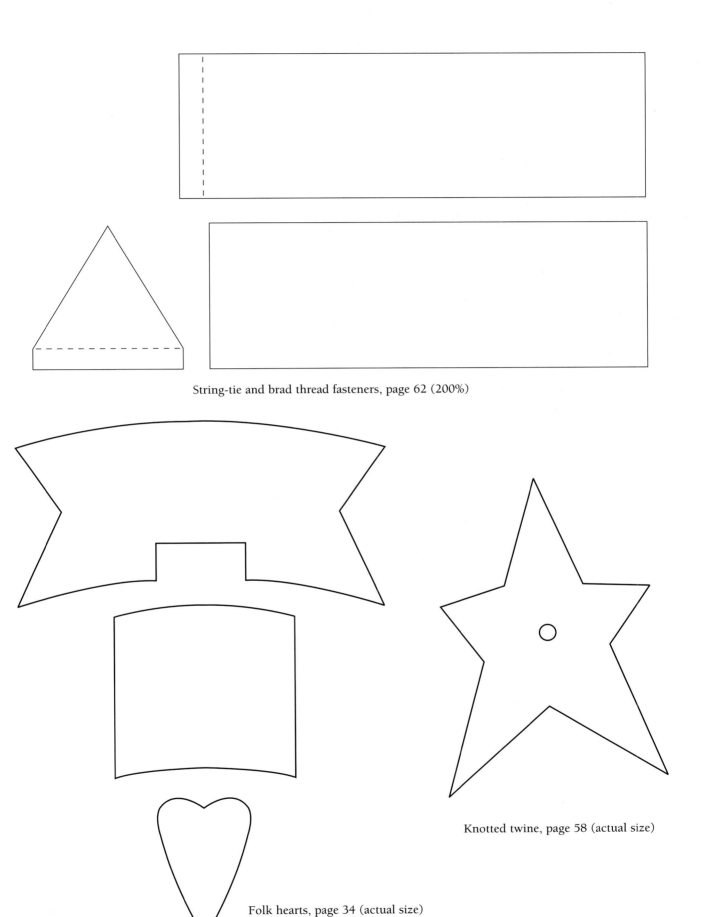

String-tie and brad thread fasteners, page 62 (200%)

Knotted twine, page 58 (actual size)

Folk hearts, page 34 (actual size)

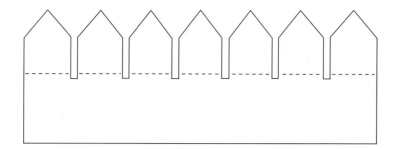

Tab-top curtains, page 78 (200%)

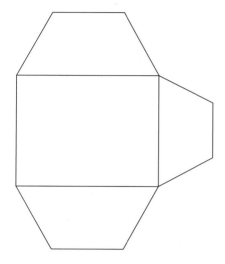

Fancy gift bags, page 80 (200%)

Border collage, page 84 (200%)

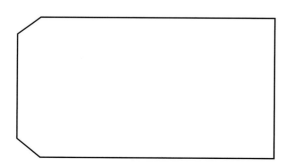

Aged tag art, page 86 (actual size)

Additional Instructions & Credits

Cover art

Encompass the four seasons with a whimsical punch art border that is duplicated in a page title and photo corners. Begin with double-matted background. For border, cut a 3" wide strip of brown paper. Cut four 2¾" squares cut from patterned cloud paper (HOTP); layer with torn strips of snow (Wubie Prints), grass (HOTP), zany zoo grass (Provo Craft) and tan paper at evenly spaced intervals to represent the four seasons. Cut five ¼" strips of wood paper (source unknown) for each seasonal square and wrap with wire to form picket fence. Mount fences atop squares, tucking picket ends behind torn paper in each scene; secure wire ends on backside with tape. Accent each seasonal scene with theme-appropriate punched shapes: mini snowflakes (winter), mini flowers (spring), small suns, mini birch leaves, hand cut stems and beads to form daisies (summer) and mini maple leaves, mini swirls, a medium apple and hand cut "straw" (autumn). Adhere scenes, evenly spaced, along border. Mat photo and journaling; adhere. Create photo corners and title in the same manner, tracing and cutting letters from pre-made "scenes" using a Pebbles in My Pocket lettering template (EK Success); adhere. Beth Rogers, Mesa, Arizona

Pages 4-5 Row Houses

Start with the pattern on page 88. Transfer pattern pieces to papers of choice; cut out. Reassemble pieces to form row house, using vellum or cut apart page protectors for window "glass." Place seasonal or theme-appropriate stickers or punched shapes behind glass. Accent house with additional seasonal or theme-appropriate embellishments such as punched shapes, stickers, curled wire, eyelets, fasteners, buttons and embroidery thread. Adhere accents with self-adhesive foam spacers for dimension, if desired. Torrey Miller, Westminster, Colorado, Inspired by Lynn Schwiebert, Osceola, Wisconsin

Page 3 Bookplate

Mat white paper with black paper; stamp with VersaMark (Tsukineko) ink using leaf stamp (Rubber Stampede). Adhere strip of double-sided adhesive along top edge, press silver metal leaf (Biblical Impressions) onto tape and use stiff brush to remove excess. Repeat on a second strip of tape with alternating assorted colors of metal leaf (Biblical Impressions). Then follow the steps on page 77 to apply different colors of metal leaf to stamped leaves to represent the four seasons. Mount along lower edge with self-adhesive foam spacers for dimension. MaryJo Regier, Littleton, Colorado

Page 6 Summertime is Family Time

Begin with a color-blocked background of red, white and blue patterned papers (Keeping Memories Alive). Then follow the instructions above to create a patriotic row house; mount on left side of page. Double mat photo, accent with curled wire and punched stars; adhere. Create matted title using a lettering template (Scrapbook Specialties), accent in same manner and mount atop decorative-scissor cut paper strip with self-adhesive foam spacers. Create a journaling block and corner accent to finish the page. Photo Greg Baron, Broomhall, Pennsylvania

Sources

The following companies manufacture products featured in this book. Please check your local retailers to find these materials. In addition, we have made every attempt to properly credit the items mentioned in this book. We apologize to any company that we have listed incorrectly or where the sources were unknown to us, and we would appreciate hearing from you.

3L Corp.
(800) 828-3130
www.3lcorp.com

3M Stationery
(800) 364-3577
www.3m.com

All My Memories
(888) 553-1998
www.allmymemories.com

All Night Media
(800) 782-6733

Anna Griffin, Inc.
(888) 817-8170
www.annagriffin.com

Art Accents
(360) 733-8989
www.artaccents.net

Art Institute Glitter Inc.
(877) 909-0805

Artistic Wire Ltd.™
(630) 530-7567
www.artisticwire.com

Avant 'Card
www.avantcard.com.au

Bazzill Basics Paper
(480) 558-8557
www.bazzillbasics.com

Beadery®, The/Greene
Plastics Corp.
(401) 539-2432

Biblical Impressions
(877) 587-0941
www.biblical.com

Blumenthal Lansing
Company
(563) 538-4211

Canson®, Inc.
(800) 628-9283

Carl Mfg. USA, Inc.
(800) 257-4771
www.carl-products.com

ChartPak
(800) 628-1910
www.chartpak.com

Close To My Heart®
(800) 655-6552
www.closetomyheart.com

Club Scrap™, Inc.
(888) 634-9100
www.clubscrap.com

Colorbök™, Inc.
(800) 366-4660
www.colorbok.com

Craf-T Products
(507) 235-3996

Creative Imaginations
(800) 942-6487
www.cigift.com

Creative Memories®
(800) 468-9335
www.creativememories.com

Creative Paperclay® Co.
(805) 484-6648
www.paperclay.com

Creative Trends
(877) 253-7687

C-Thru® Ruler Co., The
(800) 243-8419
www.cthruruler.com

Current®, Inc.
(800) 848-2848
www.currentinc.com

Daler-Rowney USA
(609) 655-5252

Darice, Inc.
(800) 321-1494
www.darice.com

Debbie Mumm®
(888) 819-2923
www.debbiemumm.com

Delta Technical Coatings,
Inc. (800) 423-4135

DMC Corp.
(973) 589-0606
www.dmc.com

DMD Industries, Inc.
(800) 805-9890
www.dmdind.com

Doodlebug Design Inc.™
(801) 966-9952

Duncan Enterprises
(559) 294-3282

EK Success™ Ltd.
(800) 524-1349
www.eksuccess.com

Ellison® Craft & Design
(800) 253-2238
www.ellison.com

Emagination Crafts, Inc.
(630) 833-9521
www.emaginationcrafts.com

Family Treasures, Inc.®
(800) 413-2645
www.familytreasures.com

Fibers By the Yard
www.fibersbytheyard.com

Fiskars, Inc.
(800) 950-0203
www.fiskars.com

Frances Meyer, Inc.®
(800) 372-6237
www.francesmeyer.com

Glue Dots International
(wholesale only)
(888) 688-7131
www.gluedots.com

Hero Art® Rubber Stamps,
Inc. (800) 822-4376
www.heroarts.com

Hot Off The Press, Inc.
(800) 227-9595
www.paperpizzaz.com

Hyglo®/AmericanPin
(800) 821-7125

Impress Rubber Stamps
(206) 901-9101
www.impressrubber-
stamps.com

Indygo Junction
(913) 341-5559
www.indygojunctioninc.com

Jesse James & Co., Inc.
(610) 435-0201

Joshuas (wholesale only)
(972) 423-1827

K1C2, LLC
(805) 676-1176

K & B Innovations
(262) 966-0305

K & Company
(888) 244-2083
www.kandcompany.com

Karen Foster Design
(801) 451-9779
www.karenfosterdesign.com

Keeping Memories Alive®
(800) 419-4949
www.scrapbooks.com

Lily Lake Crafts
(480) 659-5616
www.lilylakecrafts.com

Magenta Rubber Stamps
(800) 565-5254
www.magentarubber-
stamps.com

Magic Scraps™
(972) 385-1838
www.magicscraps.com

Making Memories
(800) 286-5263
www.makingmemories.com

Marvy® Uchida
(800) 541-5877
www.uchida.com

McGill Inc.
(800) 982-9884
www.mcgillinc.com

MiniGraphics, Inc.
(800) 442-7035

Mrs. Grossman's Paper Co.
(800) 429-4549
www.mrsgrossmans.com

Mustard Moon
(wholesale only)
(408) 229-8542
www.mustardmoon.com

Nature's Pressed
(800) 850-2499
www.naturespressed.com

On the Surface
(847) 675-2520

Paper Adventures®
(800) 727-0699
www.paperadventures.com

Paper Patch, The
(wholesale only)
(801) 253-3018
www.paperpatch.com

Plaid Enterprises, Inc.
(800) 842-4197

PrintWorks
(800) 854-6558

Provo Craft®
(888) 577-3545
www.provocraft.com

PSX Design™
(800) 782-6748
www.psxdesign.com

QuicKutz
(888) 702-1146
www.quickutz.com

Ranger Industries, Inc.
(800) 244-2211

Rocky Mountain
Scrapbook Co.
(801) 796-1471

Rubber Baby Buggy
Bumpers
(970) 224-3499

Rubber Stampede
(800) 423-4135

Sakura Hobby Craft
(310) 212-7878

Sakura of America
(800) 776-6257
www.sakuraofamerica.com

Sandylion Sticker Designs
(800) 387-4215
www.sandylion.com

Scrapbook Specialties™
(702) 456-6661
www.scrapbookspecial-
ties.com

Scrapbook Wizard™, The
(801) 947-0019

Scrap Ease®
(435) 645-0696

Scrap Pagerz
(425) 645-0696
www.scrappagerz.com

Stampa Rosa, Inc.
(800) 554-5755
www.stamparosa.com

Stampendous!®/Mark
Enterprises
(800) 869-0474
www.stampendous.com

Stampin' Up!®
(800) 782-6787
www.stampinup.com

Stampotique
(602) 862-0237
www.stampotique.com

Stickopotamus®
(888) 270-4443
www.stickopotamus.com

Sulyn Industries
(800) 257-8596
www.sulyn.com

Tsukineko®, Inc.
(800) 769-6633
www.tsukineko.com

U.S. Shell, Inc.
(956) 943-1709

Westrim Crafts®
(800) 727-2727
www.westrimcrafts.com

Wordsworth Memories
(719) 282-3495
www.wordsworthstamps.com

Wubie Prints
(888) 256-0107
www.wubieprints.com

Xyron Inc.
(800) 793-3523
www.xyron.com

Yasutomo and Company
(800) 262-6454
www.yasutomo.com

Photo Contributors

Angard, Kelly (Highlands Ranch, Colorado) Page 18

Baron, Greg (Broomhall, Pennsylvania) Page 6

Cummings, Brian (Aliso Creek, California) Page 67

Hymovitz, Patricia (Torrance, California) Page 36

Johnson, Tracy (Thornton, Colorado) Page 78

Klassen, Pam (Westminster, Colorado) Page 79

Krum, Vicki (Redmond, Washington) Page 42

Mason, Lora (Orlando, Florida) Page 39

Medlin, Catherine (Brighton, Colorado) Page 38

Rank, Michele (Cerritos, California) Page 36

Regier, MaryJo (Littleton, Colorado) Page 78

Scamfer, Sally (Bellvue, Nebraska) Page 40

Yamasaki, JoDee (Torrance, California) Page 36

Artist Index

Aho, Kathleen (Rochester, Minnesota) Page 66

Amidei, Jodi (Lafayette, Colorado) Pages 16, 52, 76

Angard, Kelly (Highlands Ranch, Colorado) Page 62

Beegle, Jenna (Woodstock, Georgia) Pages 24-25, 58

Cobb, David (Thornton, Colorado) Tree pattern Pages 84, 92

Cummings, Linda (Murfreesboro, Tennessee) Page 20

Davenport, Terri (Toledo, Ohio) Pages 32-33, 72

Frye, Pamela (Denver, Colorado) Page 46

Gallagher, Suzee (Villa Park, California) Page 50

Genovese, Sandi for Ellison Craft & Design Page 42

Ghumm, Erikia (Brighton, Colorado) Pages 38-39, 40

Ginn, Brandi (Lafayette, Colorado) Pages 66-67, 70, 87

Gosling, Joan (Keizer, Oregon) Page 14

Hayse, Marpy (Katy, Texas) Pages 54-55

Hornschu, Pam for Stampendous Pages 56-57

Klassen, Pam (Westminster, Colorado) Pages 36, 84

Magill, Teresa Page 16

Miller, Torrey (Westminster, Colorado) Pages 4-5, 60, 78-79

Monahan, Jan (Dayton, Ohio) Page 74

Morris, Tricia for Club Scrap Page 82

Ramsaroop, Nicole Hinrichs (Horst, The Netherlands) Pages 34, 44, 80-81

Regier, MaryJo (Littleton, Colorado) Pages 3, 22, 74

Rogers, Beth (Mesa, Arizona) Cover art, Pages 64-65

Sammarco, Betsy Bell (New Canaan, Connecticut) Pages 26, 86

Schoepf, Megan (Panama City, Florida) Pages 18-19

Schwiebert, Lynn (Osceola, Wisconsin) Pages 4-5

Stringer, Anissa (Phoenix, Arizona) Pages 28-29

Swords, Dana (Fredericksburg, Virginia) Page 52

Index

If you liked the techniques featured in this book, you're going to love these other great Memory Makers books! Check for them at your local bookstore, craft store or on the Internet at www.memorymakersmagazine.com.

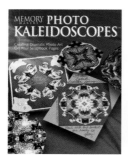